室内五人制足球竞赛规则 2014/2015

中国足球协会 审定

人民体育出版社

由国际足球联合会出版。

国际足联大街20号，8044，苏黎世，瑞士。

此规则在不同语言版本解释过程中如有歧义，以英文版文本为准。

国际足球联合会

主　席：约瑟夫S. 布拉特（瑞士）
秘书长：杰罗姆·瓦尔克（法国）
地　址：FIFA–Strasse 20, P.O. Box, 8044 Zurich, Switzerland
电　话：+41 (0)43 222 7777
传　真：+41 (0)43 222 7878
网　址：www.FIFA.com

室内五人制足球委员会

主　　席：	Worawi Makudi	泰国
执行主席：	Eugenio Figueredo	乌拉圭
成　　员：	Jilong Zhang	中国
	Petr Fousek	捷克
	Álvaro Melo Filho	巴西
	Rafael Tinoco	危地马拉
	Hans Boll	荷兰
	Ali Kafashian	伊朗
	Vitor Lup Kwan Cheung	中国澳门
	Antonio Escribano	西班牙
	Rignaal Francisca	库拉索
	Ruben Hayrapetyan	亚美尼亚
	Magdi Shams Eldin	苏丹
	Quoc Tuan Tran	越南
	Ilcho Gjorgjioski	马其顿
	Yildirim Demiroren	土耳其
	Raymond Guishard	安圭拉
	Raymond Tim Kee	特立尼达和多巴哥

Rolando Lopez Sanders	尼加拉瓜
Domingo Mituy	赤道几内亚
Anwar Altashani	利比亚
Jules Hmeun	新喀里多尼亚
Juneidi Tilmo	埃塞俄比亚

前　言

为了适应室内五人制足球运动的发展，国际足联室内五人制足球委员会近年不断对室内五人制足球竞赛规则进行修订。2014年6月30日，国际足联秘书长瓦尔克先生亲自签发了国际足联第1432号公告，即《室内五人制足球竞赛规则》2012/2013版本的修订与勘误。2014年9月，国际足联正式发布了《室内五人制足球竞赛规则》2014/2015版。

与2012/2013版室内五人制足球竞赛规则相比，2014/2015新版规则中最显著的修改是明确了替换球员时手递手交换替补背心的规则，以及更改了对加时赛每半场的时间要求和罚球点球决胜负的人数规定。为了尽快组织对室内五人制足球新规则的学习与推广实施，我们翻译出版了2014/2015中英文对照版本的《室内五人制足球竞赛规则》。

需要指出的是，国际足联室内五人制足球委员会提请各会员协会及洲际联合会注意，按照国际足联章程，确保在所有比赛中严格和统一遵守《室内五人制足球竞赛规则》是他们的职责所在。无论是规则十七章条款还是“室内五人制足球竞赛规则诠释及裁判员指南”，两部分内容在本质上毫无疑问是强制性的。

《室内五人制足球竞赛规则》2014/2015中英文对照版由中国足球协会翻译并审定，其间，中国足球协会室内五人制和沙滩足球委员会秘书长滕安军先生对本书的编辑出版给予了大力协助和支持，此外，李志中、安然、刘剑桥等同志参与了本书的翻译和校对等工作。

Content

目　录

NOTES ON THE FUTSAL LAWS OF THE GAME

Modifications

Subject to the agreement of the member association concSubject to the agreement of the member association concerned and provided that the principles of these Laws are maintained, the Laws may be modified in their application for matches for players of under 16 years of age, for women footballers, for veteran footballers (over 35 years of age) and for players with disabilities.

Any or all of the following modifications are permissible:

- size of the pitch
- size, weight and material of the ball
- width between the goalposts and height of the crossbar from the ground
- duration of the periods of play
- substitutions

Further modifications are only allowed with the consent of the FIFA Refereeing Department and the approval of the FIFA Futsal Committee.

N.B. Terms referring to natural persons are applicable to both genders.

Key

The following symbol is used in the Futsal Laws of the Game:
A single line in the margin indicates new Law changes.

室内五人制足球竞赛规则注解

修订

在确保不违背规则的前提下，经各国会员协会同意，可以对规则某些条款做适当修改，以适应16岁以下运动员、女子足球运动员、老年足球运动员（大于35岁）和残疾运动员比赛。

允许对以下各项进行修改：

- 比赛场地大小。
- 比赛用球的大小、重量和材质。
- 两门柱间宽度及球门横梁到地面的高度。
- 比赛时间。
- 替换队员人数。

如要做进一步修改，则需经国际足联裁判委员会以及国际足联室内五人制足球委员会许可。

注意：规则条款提及的自然人，同时适用于男性和女性。

说明

“|”竖线表示新修订条款

Pitch surface

Matches should be played on flat, smooth and non-abrasive surfaces, preferably made of wood or artificial material, according to the rules of the competition. Concrete or tarmac should be avoided.

Artificial turf pitches are permitted in exceptional cases and only for domestic competitions.

Pitch markings

The pitch must be rectangular and marked with lines. These lines belong to the areas of which they are boundaries and must be clearly distinguishable from the colour of the pitch.

The two longer boundary lines are called touch lines. The two shorter lines are called goal lines.

The pitch is divided into two halves by a halfway line, which joins the midpoints of the two touch lines.

The centre mark is indicated at the midpoint of the halfway line. A circle with a radius of 3m is marked around it.

A mark must be drawn outside the pitch, 5m from the corner arc and at right angles to the goal line, to ensure that defending players retreat this distance when a corner kick is being taken. The width of this mark is 8cm.

场地表面

根据竞赛规程，比赛应在表面平坦、光滑而不粗糙的场地上进行，并且场地表面最好用木材或人造材料制成。应避免使用混凝土或柏油表面。

人造草皮场地只在特殊情况下允许使用，且仅限于国内比赛。

场地标记

比赛场地必须为长方形并且用线标明。这些画线属于其标示区域的一部分，并且必须明显区别于场地颜色。

两条较长的边界线叫边线，两条较短的线叫球门线。

比赛场地被中线划分为两个半场，中线与两条边线的中点相交。

在中线的中点做一个中心标记，以其为圆心、3米为半径画一个圆圈。

在比赛场地外，距离角球弧5米且垂直于球门线处做一个标记，以保证在踢角球时守方队员能遵守规定的距离。此标记的宽度为8厘米。

Two additional marks, each at a distance of 5m to the left and the right of the second penalty mark, must be made on the pitch to indicate the minimum distance to be retreated when a kick is being taken from the second penalty mark. The width of this mark is 8 cm.

在距两个第二罚球点左右5米处的场地上必须标明另外两个标记，以明确在从第二罚球点罚球时队员退后的最小距离，此标记的宽度为8厘米。

Dimensions

The length of the touch line must be greater than the length of the goal line.

All lines must be 8cm wide.

For non-international matches, the dimensions are as follows:

Length (touch line):	minimum	25m
	maximum	42m
Width (goal line):	minimum	16m
	maximum	25m

For international matches, the dimensions are as follows:

Length (touch line):	minimum	38m
	maximum	42m
Width (goal line):	minimum	20m
	maximum	25m

场地度量

边线的长度必须大于球门线的长度。

所有画线的宽度必须为8厘米。

非国际比赛的度量如下：

长度（边线）：	最小	25米
	最大	42米
宽度（球门线）：	最小	16米
	最大	25米

国际比赛的度量如下：

长度（边线）：	最小	38米
	最大	42米
宽度（球门线）：	最小	20米
	最大	25米

The penalty area

Two imaginary lines of 6m in length are drawn from the outside of each goalpost and at right angles to the goal line; at the end of these lines a quarter circle is drawn in the direction of the nearest touch line, each with a radius of 6m from the outside of the goalpost. The upper part of each quarter circle is joined by a line 3.16m in length running parallel to the goal line between the goalposts. The area bounded by these lines and the goal line is the penalty area.

Within each penalty area, a penalty mark is made 6m from the midpoint between the goalposts and equidistant to them.

The second penalty mark

A second mark is made 10m from the midpoint between the goalposts and equidistant to them.

The corner arc

A quarter circle with a radius of 25cm from each corner is drawn inside the pitch.

罚球区

从两球门柱外沿并垂直于球门线向场内画两条长度为6米的假想线。在这条线的末端，以6米为半径从球门柱的外沿朝最近的边线方向画一个四分之一圆。两个四分之一圆的上部与一段长3.16米的直线相连接，此直线与球门线平行。由这些线和球门线围成的区域，即为罚球区。

在两个罚球区内，从两球门柱之间的中点，垂直于球门线向场内6米处标记一个罚球点，该罚球点与两球门柱等距。

第二罚球点

从两球门柱之间的中点，垂直于球门线向场内量10米做一个标记，为第二罚球点。

角球弧

在比赛场地内，以距每个角25厘米为半径画一个四分之一圆。

Goals

A goal must be placed on the centre of each goal line.

A goal consists of two upright posts equidistant from the corners and joined at the top by a horizontal crossbar. The goalposts and crossbar must be made of wood, metal or other approved material. They must be square, rectangular, round or elliptical in shape and must not be dangerous to players.

The distance (inside measurement) between the posts is 3m and the distance from the lower edge of the crossbar to the ground is 2 m.

Both goalposts and the crossbar have the same width and depth, 8 cm. The nets must be made of hemp, jute or nylon or other approved material and are attached to the back of the goalposts and the crossbar with a suitable means of support. They must be properly supported and must not interfere with the goalkeeper.

The goalposts and crossbars must be of a different colour from the pitch.

The goals must have a stabilising system that prevents them from overturning. Portable goals may only be used if they satisfy this requirement.

球门

球门必须放置在每条球门线的中央。

球门由两根等距于两个角且直竖的门柱并与其顶部的一水平横梁连接组成。球门柱和横梁必须由木头、金属或者其他被许可的材质制成。它们必须为方形、长方形、圆形或椭圆形并且不会危及运动员。

两根球门柱（内侧）之间的距离为3米，从横梁的下沿至地面的距离为2米。

两门柱和横梁的宽度与厚度相同，均为8厘米。球门网必须由大麻、黄麻、尼龙或其他被许可的材料制成，系在球门柱及横梁的后部，用适当的方式做支撑。球门网必须合理地被撑起来并不得妨碍守门员。

球门柱和横梁的颜色必须与比赛场地颜色不同。

球门必须有固定系统以防止翻到。可以使用移动球门，但仅可在满足以上要求的情况下使用。

The substitution zones

The substitution zones are the areas on the touch line in front of the team benches, the purpose of which is described in Law 3.

- They are situated in front of the technical area and are 5m in length. They are marked at each end with a line 80cm in length, 40cm of which is drawn on the pitch and 40cm off the pitch, and 8cm wide
- The area in front of the timekeeper's table 5m to either side of the halfway line is kept clear
- A team's substitution zone is situated in the half of the pitch defended by said team and changes in the second half of the match and periods of extra time, if any

替换区

替换区设在双方比赛队替补席前面的边线外。替换区的作用在第三章中详述。

- 两替换区分别位于技术区域前，长度为5米。由两条长80厘米、宽8厘米的直线标记，其中40厘米在场内、40厘米在场外。
- 替换区位于计时台前距中线两侧各5米处，且保持畅通。
- 球队的替换区位于该队防守半场一侧，在比赛下半场或加时赛下半场须交换。

Pitch

Pitch dimensions

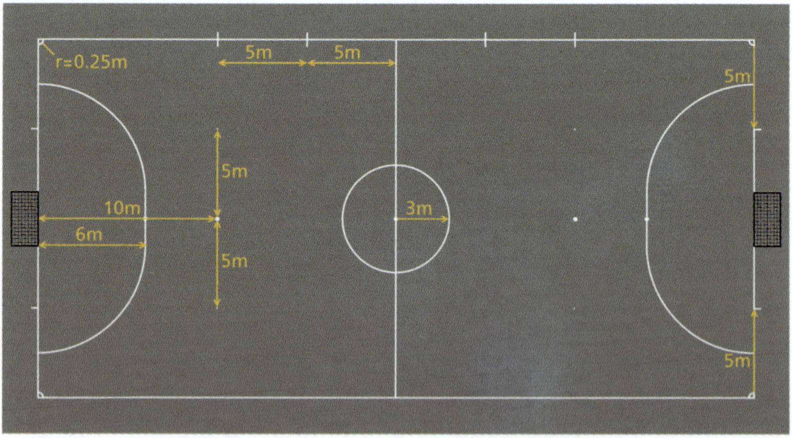

比赛场地

场地度量

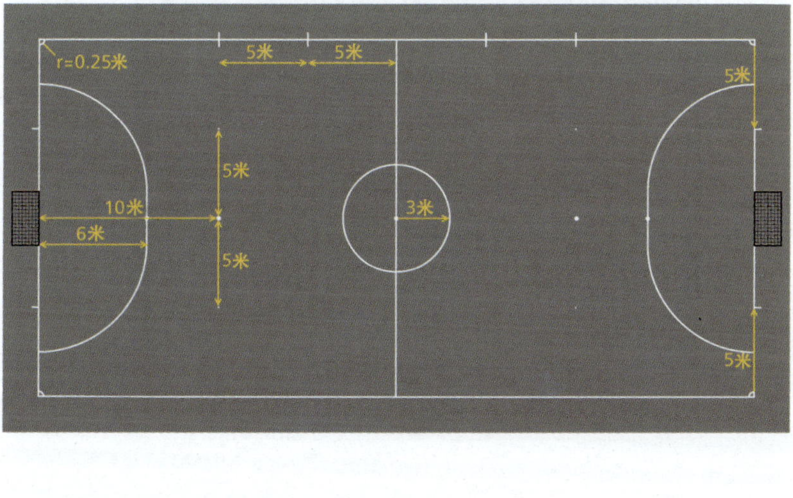

Penalty area

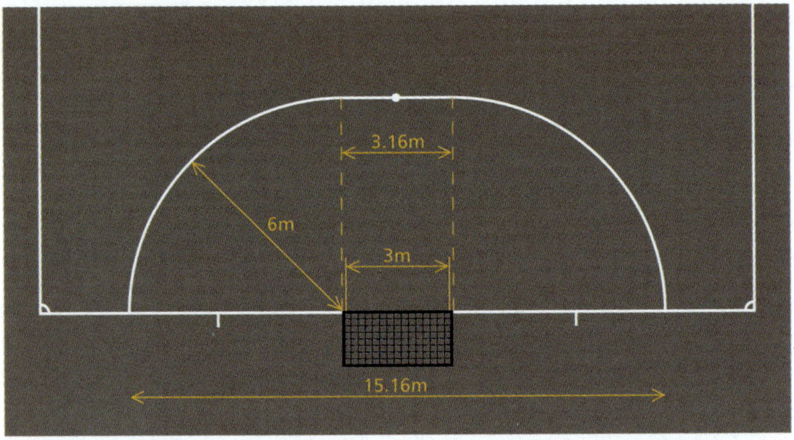

Goal

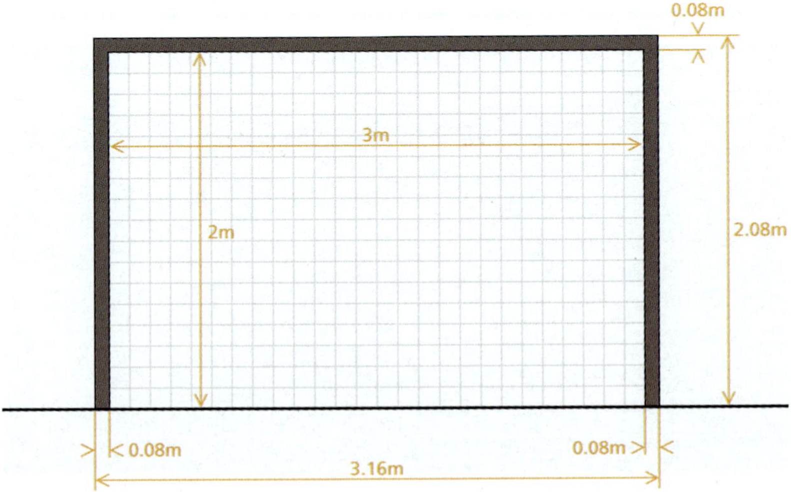

罚球区

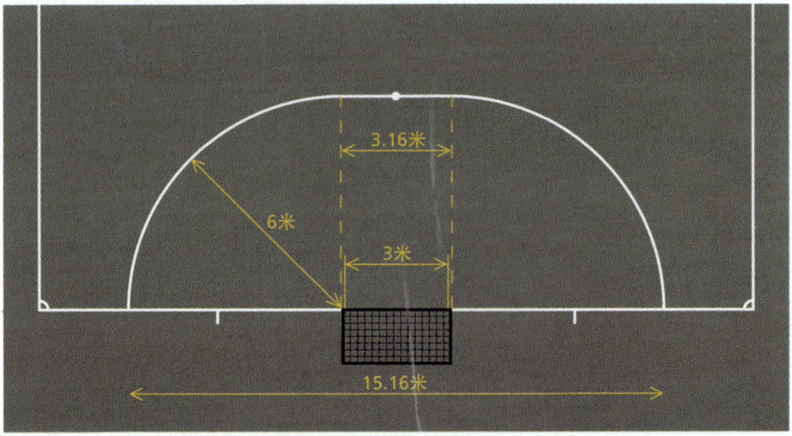

球门

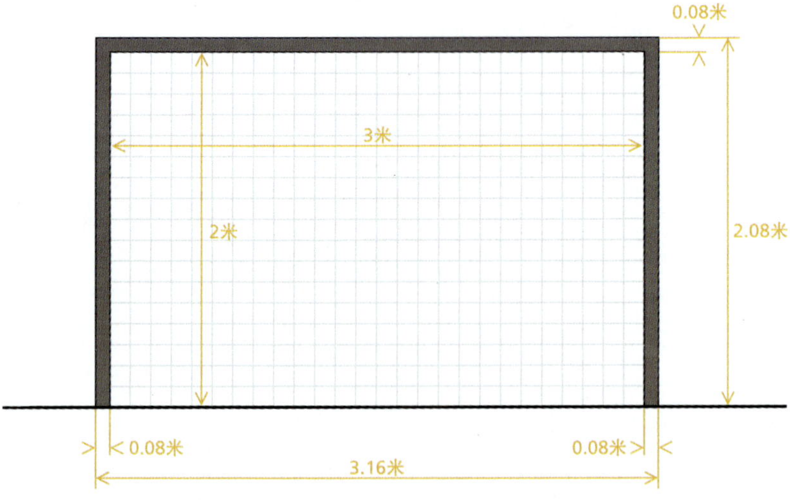

Substitution zone and technical area

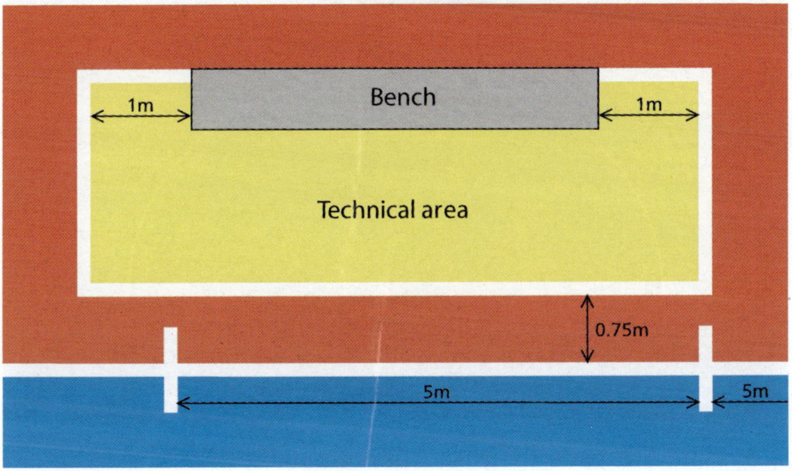

Decision 1

The technical area must meet the requirements contained in the section entitled "The Technical Area".

替换区和技术区域

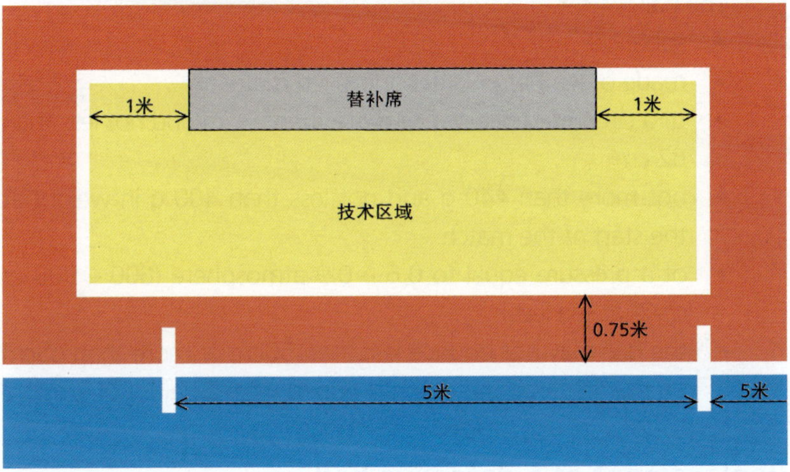

决议一

技术区域必须符合“技术区域”章节所述的要求。

Qualities and measurements

The ball is:

- spherical
- made of leather or other approved material
- of a circumference of not more than 64cm and not less than 62 cm
- not more than 440 g and not less than 400 g in weight at the start of the match
- of a pressure equal to 0.6 – 0.9 atmosphere (600 – 900 g/cm2) at sea level
- the ball may not bounce less than 50cm or more than 65cm on the first rebound when dropped from a height of 2 m

Replacement of a defective ball

If the ball bursts or becomes defective during the course of a match, the match is stopped.

- The match is restarted by dropping the replacement ball at the place where the original ball became defective, unless play was stopped inside the penalty area, in which case one of the referees drops the replacement ball on the penalty area line at the point nearest to where the original ball was located when play was stopped
- The match is restarted by retaking the kick if the ball bursts or becomes defective while a direct free kick without a wall, a kick from the second penalty mark or a kick from the penalty mark is being taken and does not touch the goalposts, the crossbar or a player and no infringement is committed

质量和测量

球:

- 圆形。
- 用皮革或其他被许可的材料制成。
- 圆周不小于62厘米、不大于64厘米。
- 在比赛开始时重量不小于400克、不大于440克。
- 气压相当于海平面0.6~0.9个大气压力（600~900克/平方厘米）。
- 当球从2米的高度下落，其初次反弹的高度应不低于50厘米或高于65厘米。

破损球的更换

如果球在比赛过程中破裂或损坏，则停止比赛：

- 用新球在原先球破损时所在地点以坠球方式重新开始比赛，除非比赛停止时球在罚球区内，在这种情况下，应由其中一名裁判员在距球破损位置最近的罚球区线上，用新球以坠球方式重新开始比赛。
- 如果球在踢无人墙的直接任意球、第二罚球点罚球或者罚球点球踢出的过程中破裂或损坏，在这个过程中球没有触及球门柱、横梁或队员，且没有犯规发生的情况下，则应重踢。

If the ball bursts or becomes defective while not in play (at a kick-off, goal clearance, corner kick, dropped ball, free kick, penalty kick or ball inbound):

- the match is restarted in accordance with the Futsal Laws of the Game

The ball may not be changed during the match without the authority of the referees.

如果球在开球、掷球门球、角球、坠球、任意球、罚球点球或踢界外球等比赛停止时破裂或损坏：

- 按照室内五人制足球竞赛规则相应的规定重新开始比赛。

在比赛中未经裁判员允许，不得更换比赛用球。

Advertising

In matches played in an official competition organised under the auspices of FIFA, the confederations or the member associations, no form of commercial advertising on the ball is permitted, except for the emblem of the competition, the name of the competition organiser and the authorised trademark of the manufacturer. The name of the competition regulations may restrict the size and number of such markings.

广告

在国际足联、洲际联合会和国家协会主办的比赛中，除了比赛及比赛组织者的徽标和授权制造商的商标外，不允许在球上出现任何形式的商业广告。竞赛规程可限制此类标志的尺寸和数量。

Players

A match is played by two teams, each consisting of not more than five players, one of whom is the goalkeeper.

A match may not start if either team consists of fewer than three players.

The match is abandoned if one of the teams has fewer than three players on the pitch.

Official competitions

Up to a maximum of nine substitutes may be used in any match played in an official competition organised under the auspices of FIFA, the confederations or the member associations. The rules of the competition must state how many substitutes may be nominated, up to a maximum of nine.

The number of substitutions that may be made during a match is unlimited.

Other matches

In national "A" team matches, up to a maximum of ten substitutes may be used. In all other matches, a greater number of substitutes may be used, provided that:

- the teams concerned reach agreement on a maximum number

队员

一场比赛应有两队参加，每队上场球员不得多于5人，其中1人必须为守门员。

如果任何一队少于3人则比赛不能开始。

在比赛中，任何一队在场上队员人数少于3人，比赛将被终止。

正式比赛

在由国际足联、洲际联合会或国家协会主办的任何正式比赛中，每场比赛最多可以使用9名替补队员。竞赛规程必须对替补队员的提名人数做出规定，但不多于9人。

比赛中替换队员次数不受限制。

其他比赛

在国家A级比赛中，最多可使用10名替补队员。在其他所有比赛中，只要符合下列条件即可使用更多数量的替补队员：

- 比赛双方就替补队员人数达成一致。

- the referees are informed before the match

If the referees are not informed, or if no agreement is reached before the match, no more than ten substitutes are allowed.

All matches

In all matches, the names of the players and substitutes must be given to the referees prior to the start of the match, whether they are present or not. Any substitute whose name is not given to the referees at this time may not take part in the match.

Substitution procedure

A substitution may be made at any time, whether the ball is in play or not. To replace a player with a substitute, the following conditions must be observed:

- The player leaves the pitch via his own team's substitution zone, save in the exceptions provided for in the Futsal Laws of the Game
- The substitute only enters the pitch after the player being replaced has left
- The substitute enters the pitch via his own team's substitution zone
- The substitution is completed when a substitute enters the pitch via his own team's substitution zone, after handing the bib to the player being replaced, unless this player has had to leave the pitch via another zone for any reason provided for in the Laws of the Game, in which case the substitute shall hand his bib to the third referee

- 比赛前通知裁判员。

如果赛前没有通知裁判员，或双方未达成一致，替补队员人数不得超过10人。

所有比赛

在所有比赛中，无论队员或替补队员是否在场，他们的名单必须在比赛开始前交给裁判员。任何未及时提名的替补队员不能参加本场比赛。

替补程序

无论在比赛进行或停止时，队员可在任何时候进行替换。替换队员时必须遵守以下规定：

- 除室内五人制足球竞赛规则规定的特例外，队员需经本队替换区离场。
- 替补队员只能在被替换队员已经离场的情况下方可进入场地。
- 替补队员需经本方替换区进入场地。
- 当替补队员经本方替换区进入场地即完成了替补程序，在此之前他需要将背心交给被替换队员；除非被替换队员依据竞赛规则中的任何原因从其他区域离场，在这种情况下，替补队员应将背心交给第三裁判员。

- From that moment, the substitute becomes a player and the player he has replaced becomes a substituted player
- The substituted player may take further part in the match
- All substitutes are subject to the authority and jurisdiction of the referees, whether called upon to play or not
- If a period is extended to allow a penalty kick, a kick from the second penalty mark or a direct free kick without a wall to be taken, only the goalkeeper of the defending team may be substituted

Changing the goalkeeper

- Any of the substitutes may change places with the goalkeeper without informing the referees or waiting for a stoppage in the match
- Any player may change places with the goalkeeper
- The player changing places with the goalkeeper must do so during a stoppage in the match and must inform the referees before the change is made
- A player or substitute replacing the goalkeeper must wear a goalkeeper's jersey with his number on the back

- 从那时起，替补队员成为场上队员，被替换队员成为替补队员。
- 被替换队员可再次参加该场比赛。
- 所有替补队员无论上场与否，裁判员均有权对其行使职权。
- 如果半场比赛被延长至允许执行完罚球点球、第二罚球点罚球或者踢无人墙的直接任意球，此时只有防守方的守门员允许被替换。

更换守门员

- 比赛中任何替补队员都可替换守门员，而无需通知裁判员或等待比赛停止。
- 任何场上队员可与守门员互换位置。
- 场上队员和守门员互换位置必须在比赛停止时进行，并且必须在换位前通知裁判员。
- 场上队员或替补队员替换守门员必须穿着守门员服装且背后有其本人的号码。

Infringements and sanctions

If a substitute enters the pitch before the player being replaced has left or, during a substitution, a substitute enters the pitch from a place other than his team's substitution zone:

- the referees stop play (although not immediately if they can apply the advantage)
- the referees caution him for infringing the substitution procedure and order him to leave the pitch

If the referees have stopped play, it is restarted with an indirect free kick to the opposing team from the position of the ball at the time of the stoppage (see Law 13 – Position of free kick). If this substitute or his team also commits another infringement, play is restarted in accordance with the section entitled "Interpretation of the Futsal Laws of the Game and Guidelines for Referees" (Law 3).

If, during a substitution, the player being replaced leaves the pitch for reasons not provided for in the Futsal Laws of the Game and via a place other than his team's substitution zone:

- the referees stop play (although not immediately if they can apply the advantage)
- the referees caution the player for infringing the substitution procedure

If the referees have stopped play, it is restarted with an indirect free kick to the opposing team from the position of the ball at the time of the stoppage (see Law 13 – Position of free kick).

违规与判罚

如果替补队员在被替换队员还未完全离场前进入比赛场地，或在替换过程中替补队员从本队替换区外进入场地：

- 裁判员停止比赛（当掌握有利时不必立即停止比赛）。
- 裁判员黄牌警告违反替补程序的队员，并要求其离场。

如果裁判员已经停止比赛，应由对方在比赛停止时球所在地点踢间接任意球重新开始比赛（参见规则第十三章–任意球的位置）。如果该替补队员或其球队还有其他违规，比赛则根据本规则中“室内五人制足球竞赛规则诠释及裁判员指南”（第三章）的规定重新开始比赛。

如果在替换队员时，被替换队员因非室内五人足球竞赛规则允许的原因离开场地，或没有经过本方球队替换区：

- 裁判员停止比赛（当掌握有利时不必立即停止比赛）。
- 裁判员黄牌警告违反替补程序的队员。

如果裁判员已经停止比赛，应由对方在比赛停止时球所在地点踢间接任意球重新开始比赛（参见规则第十三章–任意球的位置）。

In the event of any other infringements of this Law:

- the players concerned are cautioned
- the match is restarted with an indirect free kick to the opposing team from the position of the ball at the time of the stoppage (see Law 13 – Position of free kick). In special cases, play is restarted in accordance with the section entitled "Interpretation of the Futsal Laws of the Game and Guidelines for Referees" (Law 3)

其他任何违反本章规则的违规行为：

- 相关队员将被警告。
- 应由对方在比赛停止时球所在地点踢间接任意球重新开始比赛（参见规则第十三章—任意球的位置）。在特殊情况下，比赛应根据本规则中“室内五人制足球竞赛规则诠释和裁判员指南”（第三章）的规定重新开始比赛。

Players and substitutes sent off

A player who has been sent off before the kick-off may be replaced only by one of the named substitutes.

A named substitute who has been sent off, either before the kick-off or after play has started, may not be replaced.

A substitute player may replace a sent-off player and enter the pitch after two minutes of playing time have elapsed since the sending-off, provided that he has the authorisation of the timekeeper or the third referee (assistant referees), unless a goal is scored before the two minutes have elapsed, in which case the following conditions apply:

- If there are five players against four and the team with the greater number of players scores a goal, the team with only four players may be completed with a fifth player
- If both teams are playing with three or four players and a goal is scored, both teams remain with the same number of players
- If there are five players playing against three, or four against three, and the team with the greater number of players scores a goal, the team with three players may be increased by one player only
- If the team that scores the goal is the one with fewer players, the game continues without changing the number of players

队员和替补队员被罚令出场

队员在开球前被罚令出场，只可从提名的替补队员中选1人替换。

凡被提名的替补队员被罚令出场，无论是在开球前或在比赛开始后，均不得替换。

只有当计时员或第三裁判员（两者统称助理裁判员）允许的情况下，替补队员在被罚令出场的队员被罚出场两分钟后方可进入比赛场地。如果在两分钟内有进球发生，则应适用以下条款：

- 如果比赛当时5对4，并且人数较多的一方进球，则4人一方的球队应补齐第5名队员。
- 如果比赛当时双方均为3人或4人并有进球发生，则比赛双方保持原有人数不变。
- 如果比赛当时为5对3或者4对3，并且人数较多一方进球，则3人一方球队只可增加1人。
- 如果人数较少一方进球，则不改变队员人数继续进行比赛。

Safety

A player must not use equipment or wear anything that is dangerous to himself or another player (including any kind of jewellery).

Basic equipment

The basic compulsory equipment of a player comprises the following separate items:

- A jersey or shirt – if undergarments are worn, the colour of the sleeve must be the same main colour as the sleeve of the jersey or shirt
- Shorts – if undershorts are worn, they must be of the same main colour as the shorts. The goalkeeper is permitted to wear long trousers
- Stockings: if tape or similar material is applied externally it must be the same colour as that part of the stocking it is applied to
- Shinguards
- Footwear – canvas or soft leather training or gymnastic shoes with soles of rubber or a similar material

Shinguards

- are covered entirely by the stockings
- are made of rubber, plastic or a similar approved material
- provide a reasonable degree of protection

安全性

队员不得使用、佩戴可能危及自己及其他队员的装备或任何物件（包括各种珠宝饰物）。

基本装备

队员必需的基本装备包括下列相互分离的部分：

- 运动上衣—如穿紧身内衣，其袖子的颜色应与运动上衣袖子的主色相同。
- 运动短裤—如穿紧身内裤，必须与短裤的主色相同。守门员可以穿长裤。
- 护袜—如果需要额外使用胶带或相似材料，则其颜色应与球袜被覆盖部分的颜色相同。
- 护腿板。
- 足球鞋—帆布、软皮面训练鞋或体操鞋，鞋底为橡胶或类似材质。

护腿板

- 必须由护袜完全包住。
- 由橡胶、塑料或类似被许可的材质制成。
- 提供适当程度的保护。

Colours

- The two teams must wear colours that distinguish them from each other and also the referees and the assistant referees
- Each goalkeeper must wear colours that distinguish him from the other players, the referees and the assistant referees

Infringements and sanctions

In the event of any infringement of this Law:

- play need not be stopped
- the player at fault is instructed by the referees to leave the pitch to correct his equipment when the ball next ceases to be in play, unless he has already corrected his equipment
- any player required to leave the pitch to correct his equipment must not re-enter without the permission of the referees or third referee
- the referees, either directly or through the third referee, check that the player's equipment is correct before allowing him to re-enter the pitch
- the player, if he has not been substituted, is only allowed to re-enter the pitch when the ball is out of play or under the supervision of the third referee when the ball is in play

颜色

- 比赛两队的着装颜色必须有别于对方和裁判员及助理裁判员。
- 每名守门员的服装颜色必须有别于其他队员、裁判员和助理裁判员。

违规与判罚

对于任何违反本章规则的：

- 比赛不需要停止。
- 裁判员指出场上队员的装备有问题后，该队员应在比赛下一次停止时离开比赛场地去调整装备，除非该队员已经调整好装备。
- 任何被要求离开比赛场地调整装备的队员，在未经裁判员或者第三裁判员的允许不得再次进场。
- 在允许队员重新进入场地之前，裁判员需直接或者通过第三裁判员检查该队员装备。
- 如果该队员没有被替换下场，他只能在比赛停止时或比赛进行状态中在第三裁判员的监督下重新进入场地。

A player having been required to leave the pitch because of an infringement of this Law and not having been substituted who re-enters the pitch without the permission of the referees or third referee must be cautioned.

Restart of play

If play is stopped by the referees to administer a caution:

- the match is restarted with an indirect free kick taken by a player of the opposing team, from the place where the ball was located when the referees stopped the match (see Law 13 – Position of free kick)

Advertising on equipment

Basic compulsory equipment

The basic compulsory equipment must not have any political, religious or personal slogans, images or statements. The team of a player whose basic compulsory equipment has political, religious or personal slogans, images or statements will be sanctioned by the competition organizer or by FIFA.

Undergarments

Players must not reveal undergarments showing political, religious or personal slogans, images or statements, or any advertising other than the manufacturer's logo.

Players or teams revealing undergarments showing political, religious or personal slogans, images or statements or advertising other than the manufacturer's logo will be sanctioned by the competition organizer or by FIFA.

队员因违反本规则而被要求离开比赛场地，且并未被替换下场，在未获得裁判员或第三裁判员允许时重新进入场地必须被警告。

重新开始比赛

如果裁判员停止比赛执行警告：

- 由对方球队在比赛停止时球所在地点踢间接任意球重新开始比赛（参见规则第十三章—任意球的位置）。

装备上的广告

基本装备

基本装备不得有任何涉及政治、宗教和个人的标语、图片或言论。基本装备带有政治、宗教和个人的标语、图片或言论的队员所在球队将受到比赛组织者或国际足联的处罚。

贴身内衣

队员不得暴露带有政治、宗教和个人的标语、图片或言论，以及除制造商标识以外广告的贴身内衣。

队员或球队暴露带有政治、宗教和个人的标语、图片或言论，以及除制造商标识以外广告的贴身内衣将受到比赛组织者或国际足联的处罚。

The authority of the referees

Each match is controlled by two referees, the referee and the second referee, who have full authority to enforce the Futsal Laws of the Game in connection with the match to which they have been appointed.

Powers and duties

The referees:

- enforce the Futsal Laws of the Game
- control the match in cooperation with the assistant referees, where applicable
- ensure that any ball used meets the requirements of Law 2
- ensure that the players' equipment meets the requirements of Law 4
- keep a record of the match
- stop the match, at their discretion, for any infringements of the Futsal Laws of the Game
- stop the match because of outside interference of any kind
- stop the match if, in their opinion, a player is seriously injured and ensure that he is removed from the pitch. An injured player may only return to the pitch after the match has restarted
- allow play to continue until the ball is out of play if a player is, in their opinion, only slightly injured
- ensure that any player bleeding from a wound leaves the pitch. The player may only return on receiving a signal from the referees, who must be satisfied, either directly or through the third referee, that the bleeding has stopped

裁判员的权力

每场比赛由两名裁判员控制，即裁判员和第二裁判员。他们在被任命的比赛中具有全部权力去执行与比赛相关的室内五人制足球竞赛规则。

权限和职责

裁判员：

- 执行室内五人制足球竞赛规则。
- 在有助理裁判员的情况下，与其尽可能合作控制比赛。
- 确保任何比赛用球符合规则第二章的要求。
- 确保队员装备符合规则第四章的要求。
- 对比赛进行记录。
- 根据判断，当任何违反规则的行为发生时停止比赛。
- 因任何外界干扰停止比赛。
- 如果他认为队员受伤严重则停止比赛，并确保将其移出场外。受伤队员只能在比赛重新开始后方可重返比赛场地。
- 如果他认为队员只是受轻伤，则允许比赛继续进行直到停止。
- 确保队员因受伤流血时离开比赛场地。因流血离场的队员只有在当裁判员或第三裁判员确认流血已经停止，并在得到裁判员信号后方可重回场地。

- allow play to continue when the team against which an offence has been committed stands to benefit from such an advantage and penalise the original offence if the anticipated advantage does not ensue at that time
- punish the more serious offence when a player commits more than one offence at the same time
- punish the more serious misconduct when a player commits more than one act of misconduct at the same time
- take disciplinary action against players guilty of cautionable and sending-off offences. They are not obliged to take this action immediately but must do so when the ball next goes out of play
- take action against team officials who fail to conduct themselves in a responsible manner and may, at their discretion, expel them from the technical area and the surrounds of the pitch
- ensure that no unauthorised persons enter the pitch
- indicate the restart of the match after it has been stopped
- give the signals described in the section entitled "Referee and Assistant Referee Signals"
- position themselves on the pitch as described in the section entitled "Positioning with ball in play" and "Position in ball out of play situations", which are part of the "Interpretation of the Futsal Laws of the Game and Guidelines for Referees" (Law 5 – The Referees), when they are required to do so
- provide the appropriate authorities with a match report, which includes information on any sactions imposed on players and/or team officials and any other incidents that occurred before, during or after the match

- 当一队被犯规而根据“有利”条款能获利时，则允许比赛继续进行。如果预期的“有利”在那一时刻没有发生，则判罚最初的犯规。
- 当队员同时出现一种以上的犯规时，则对较严重的犯规进行判罚。
- 当队员同时出现一种以上的不正当行为时，则对较严重的行为进行纪律制裁。
- 对犯有可警告或罚令出场的队员采取纪律处罚。裁判员不必立即进行处罚，但必须在比赛下一次停止时进行。
- 在球队官员做出不负责任的举动时进行制止，并可酌情将其驱逐出技术区域及场地周围地区。
- 确保未经批准的人员不得进入比赛场地。
- 比赛停止后示意重新开始比赛的方式。
- 根据“裁判员和助理裁判员信号”章节的规定给予信号。
- 根据比赛需要和“室内五人制足球竞赛规则诠释及裁判员指南”（第五章—裁判员）中“比赛中选位”和“比赛停止时选位”的建议，在比赛中移动选位。
- 向相关部门提交比赛报告，包括任何针对队员或球队官员的纪律处分信息，以及任何其他在赛前、赛中或赛后发生的意外事件。

The referee:

- acts as timekeeper and third referee in the event that the assistant referees are not present
- suspends or abandons the match, at his discretion, for any infringements of the Futsal Laws of the Game
- suspends or abandons the match because of outside interference of any kind

The second referee:

- replaces the referee in the event that he becomes injured or indisposed

裁判员：

- 当助理裁判员不在场时充当第三裁判员和计时员。
- 根据其判断因违反竞赛规则停止或终止比赛。
- 因任何外界干扰停止或终止比赛。

第二裁判员：

- 当裁判员受伤或身体不适时对其进行替换。

Decisions of the referees

The decisions of the referees regarding facts connected with play, including whether or not a goal is scored and the result of the match, are final.

The referees may only change a decision on realising that it is incorrect or, at their discretion, on the advice of an assistant referee, provided that they have not restarted play or terminated the match.

The decisions of the referee prevail over those of the second referee if both signal an infringement and there is disagreement between them.

In the event of undue interference or improper conduct, the referee will relieve the second referee or the assistant referees of their duties, arrange for them to be substituted and make a report to the appropriate authorities.

Responsibilities of the referees

The referees (or where applicable, the assistant referees) are not held liable for:

- any kind of injury suffered by a player, official or spectator
- any damage to property of any kind

裁判员的决定

裁判员根据与比赛相关的事实所做出的决定，包括进球是否得分和比赛的结果是最终的决定。

只有在比赛未重新开始或终止前，裁判员可以根据自己的判断或助理裁判员的意见而改变确实不正确的决定。

当裁判员与第二裁判员就某一违规行为同时发出判罚信号，而发生双方判罚不一致时，以裁判员的判罚决定为准。

如果第二裁判员或助理裁判员过分干预或有不恰当的行为表现时，裁判员可解除其职责，并指派他人替代，并将比赛报告提交有关部门。

裁判员的责任

裁判员（同样适用于助理裁判员）对下列情况不承担法律责任：

- 队员、官员和观众任何形式的受伤。
- 任何形式的财产损坏。

- any other loss suffered by any individual, club, company, association or other body, which is due or which may be due to any decision that they may take under the terms of the Futsal Laws of the Game or in respect of the normal procedures required to hold, play and control a match

Such decisions may include:

- a decision that the condition of the pitch or its surrounds or that the weather conditions are such as to allow or not to allow a match to take place
- a decision to abandon a match for whatever reason
- a decision as to the suitability of the accessories and equipment used during a match
- a decision to stop or not to stop a match due to spectator interference or any problem in spectator areas
- a decision to stop or not to stop play to allow an injured player to be removed from the pitch for treatment
- a decision to require an injured player to be removed from the pitch for treatment
- a decision to allow or not to allow a player to wear certain apparel or equipment
- a decision (where they have the authority) to allow or not to allow any persons (including team or venue officials, security officers, photographers or other media representatives) to be present in the vicinity of the pitch
- any other decision that they may take in accordance with the Futsal Laws of the Game or in conformity with their duties under the terms of FIFA, confederation, member association or league rules or regulations under which the match is played

- 由于或者可能由于他根据室内五人制足球竞赛规则所做出的决定，或者按照正常程序要求维持、进行和控制比赛，而对任何人、俱乐部、公司、协会或类似机构所造成的任何损失。

这些决定可能包括：

- 裁判员根据比赛场地及其周边情况，或天气的影响决定比赛是否进行。
- 决定由于各种原因而中止比赛。
- 决定比赛期间适合比赛的场地器材和比赛用球。
- 由于观众的影响或观众席中的任何问题，决定是否停止比赛。
- 决定是否停止比赛而允许受伤队员移出比赛场地接受治疗。
- 决定要求将受伤队员移出比赛场地接受治疗。
- 决定队员是否可以穿着某种服装或佩戴某种装备。
- 决定（在其职责范围内）是否允许任何人（包括球队或体育场官员、安保官员、摄影记者或其他新闻媒体代表）出现在比赛场地附近。
- 裁判员根据室内五人制足球竞赛规则或依照国际足联、洲际联合会、国家协会或联盟对该比赛制定的规程或规定而做出的判决。

International matches

A second referee is mandatory for international matches.

Reserve assistant referee

In tournaments or competitions where a reserve assistant referee is appointed, his role and duties must be in accordance with the provisions stipulated in the Futsal Laws of the Game.

国际比赛

国际比赛必须委派1名第二裁判员。

候补助理裁判员

如果在锦标赛和其他比赛中委派候补助理裁判员，其作用和职责必须与室内足球规则中的原则一致。

The authority of the assistant referees

Two assistant referees may be appointed (a third referee and a timekeeper) who must perform their duties in accordance with the Futsal Laws of the Game. They are positioned off the pitch, level with the halfway line and on the same side as the substitution zones. The timekeeper remains seated at the timekeeper's table, while the third referee may perform his duties either seated or standing up.

The timekeeper and the third referee are equipped with a suitable chronometer and the necessary equipment to keep a record of accumulated fouls, which is supplied by the association or club under whose jurisdiction the match is being played.

They are provided with a timekeeper's table in order to perform their duties correctly.

Powers and duties

The third referee:

- assists the referees and the timekeeper
- keeps a record of the players taking part in the match
- monitors the replacement of balls at the request of the referees
- checks the substitutes' equipment before they enter the pitch
- records the goalscorers' numbers

助理裁判员的权力

每场比赛应委派两名助理裁判员（1名第三裁判员和1名计时员），他们必须依照室内五人制足球竞赛规则行使职责。他们的位置在比赛场地外、两替换区同侧靠近中线处。计时员应就座于计时台处，同时第三裁判员则就座或站立行使职责。

应为计时员与第三裁判员配备计时器，以及可以显示累计犯规次数的设备。这些设备应由比赛场地所属协会或俱乐部提供。

应为他们提供计时台，以便于其 能够正确地行使职责。

权限和职责

第三裁判员：

- 协助两名裁判员和计时员。
- 记录参加比赛队员。
- 在裁判员的要求下监督球的更换。
- 在替补队员尚未进入比赛场地前检查其装备。
- 记录进球队员的号码。

- informs the timekeeper of a request for a time-out when a team official makes one (see Law 7 – The Duration of the Match)
- gives the mandatory time-out signal once the timekeeper has sounded the acoustic signal, to inform the referees and the teams that the time-out has been granted

- keeps a record of the time-outs requested
- keeps a record of the accumulated fouls by each team signalled by the referees in each period of play
- gives the mandatory signal that one team has committed five accumulated fouls in a period of play
- places a visible sign on the timekeeper's table to indicate that a team has committed five accumulated fouls in one period of play
- records the names and numbers of any players cautioned or sent off
- hands a document to the officials of each team before the start of each period of play with which they can request time-outs and collects it at the end of each period if none have been requested

FIFA®

For the Game. For the World.

TIME-OUT
TEMP MORT
TIEMPO MUERTO
AUSZEIT

- 当某队官员请求暂停时通知计时员（参见规则第七章—比赛时间）。
- 在计时员发出声音信号通知裁判员和球队准许比赛暂停的情况下，给出暂停信号。

- 记录暂停请求情况。
- 记录各半场比赛中裁判员示意的每队累计犯规次数。
- 任一球队在半场比赛中已累计犯规5次时给予必须的信号。
- 在计时台上摆设标志，示意某队已经在半场比赛中累计犯规5次。
- 记录任何被警告或罚令出场队员的姓名和号码。
- 在各半场比赛开始前向每队官员递交表单，以便于各队据此提出暂停请求。如果球队没有提出暂停请求，那么这些表单在各半场比赛结束后收回。

FIFA®

For the Game. For the World.

暂 停

- hands a document to the officials of each team which indicates when a substitute can enter the pitch to replace a player who has been sent off

FIFA®

For the Game. For the World.

THE SUBSTITUTE PLAYER WILL BE ABLE TO ENTER THE FIELD OF PLAY, WHEN THERE ARE -____ MINUTE(S) AND ___ SECOND(S) ON THE CHRONOMETER LEFT TO END THE ___ PERIOD.

LE JOUEUR SUBSTITUT POURRA ENTRER DANS LE TERRAIN DE JEU QUAND LE CHRONOMÈTRE INDIQUERA ___ MINUTE(S) ET ___ SECONDE(S) ___ POUR FINIR LA ___ PÉRIODE.

EL JUGADOR SUSTITUTO PODRÁ ENTRAR EN EL TERRENO DE JUEGO CUANDO EL CRONÓMETRO ESTÉ EN EL MINUTO ___ Y SEGUNDOS ___ PARA FINALIZAR EL ___ PERIODO

DER ERSATZPIELER KANN DAS SPIELFELD BETRETEN, WENN AUF DER ZEITMESSUNG NOCH ___ MINUTE(N) UND ___ SEKUNDE(N) FEHLEN, UM DIE ___ PERIODE ZU BEENDEN.

- 递交给每队官员一份表单，示意何时一名替补队员可以进入比赛场地替代另一被罚令出场队员。

FIFA

For the Game. For the World.

当计时器所示时间距_____半场结束_____分钟_____秒时，替补队员可以进入比赛场地。

- under the referees' supervision, checks the entry of a player who has left the pitch to correct his equipment
- under the referees' supervision, checks the entry of a player who has left the pitch due to an injury of any kind
- signals to the referees when an obvious error has been made in cautioning or sending off a player or if an act of violence has been committed out of their field of vision. In any case, the referees decide on any facts connected with play
- supervises the conduct of the persons situated in the technical area, if any, and on the benches and informs the referees of any inappropriate behaviour
- keeps a record of stoppages in play because of outside interference and the reasons for them
- provides any other information relevant to the game
- positions himself on the pitch as described in the section entitled "Position with ball in play" and "Positioning in ball out of play situations", which are part of the "Interpretation of the Futsal Laws of the Game and Guidelines for Referees" (Law 5 – The Referees), when he is required to do so
- replaces the second referee in the event that the referee or second referee becomes injured or indisposed

- 在裁判员的委派下，监督已经离场调整装备的队员重新进入场地。
- 在裁判员的委派下，监督由于任何受伤已经离场的队员重新进入场地。
- 在裁判员执行警告或罚令出场出现明显错误时，或有暴力行为发生在裁判员视线范围之外时，用信号通知裁判员。但无论怎样，裁判员有权决定任何与比赛有关的事项。
- 监督任何位于技术区域和替补席上人员的行为，并将他们任何不适当的行为通知裁判员。
- 记录比赛中由于外界干扰而产生的中断及其原因。
- 提供任何与比赛相关的其他信息。
- 在被要求时，能根据“室内五人制足球竞赛规则诠释和裁判员指南中的‘比赛中选位’‘比赛停止时选位’（第五章—裁判员）”的要求在比赛场地上选位。
- 当裁判员、第二裁判员受伤或不能行使职责时取代第二裁判员。

The timekeeper ensures that the duration of the match complies with the provisions of Law 7 by:

- starting the chronometer after a kick-off has been taken correctly
- stopping the chronometer when the ball is out of play
- restarting the chronometer after play has been correctly resumed after a kick-in, a goal clearance, a corner kick or kick-off, a free kick, kicks from the penalty mark or second penalty mark or a dropped ball
- recording the goals, accumulated fouls and periods of play on the public scoreboard, if available
- indicating a team's request for a time-out with a whistle or acoustic signal distinct from the one used by the referees, after the third referee has informed him
- timing the one-minute time-out
- indicating the end of the one-minute time-out with a different whistle or acoustic signal from those used by the referees
- indicating the fifth accumulated foul by a team with a different whistle or acoustic signal from the one used by the referees, after the third referee has informed him
- timing a player's two-minute expulsion
- indicating the end of the first half, the end of the match or the end of the periods of extra time, if any, with a different whistle or acoustic signal from the one used by the referees

计时员确保比赛时间与规则第七章相符：

- 当比赛正确开球后开启计时器。
- 当比赛停止时停止计时器。
- 当比赛经踢界外球、掷球门球、角球、中圈开球、任意球、从罚球点或第二罚球点踢出或坠球重新开始比赛后，开启计时器计时。
- 在可能的情况下在计分板上公开记录的进球、累计犯规和比赛节次。
- 在得到第三裁判员通知后，以不同于裁判员的哨音或其他声音信号示意某队要求暂停。
- 对1分钟暂停进行计时。
- 以不同于裁判员的哨音或其他声音信号示意1分钟暂停结束。
- 在得到第三裁判员通知后，以不同于裁判员的哨音或其他声音信号示意某队第5次累计犯规。
- 负责罚令队员出场2分钟的计时。
- 以不同于裁判员的哨音或声音信号，示意上半场、全场及加时赛半场时间结束。

- positions himself on the pitch as described in the section entitled "Position with ball in Play" and "Positioning in ball out of play situations", which are part of the "Interpretation of the Futsal Laws of the Game and Guidelines for Referees" (Law 5 – The Referees), when he is required to do so
- performs the specific duties of the third referee in the event of the latter's absence
- provides any other information relevant to the game

International matches

For international matches, the presence of a third referee and a timekeeper is mandatory.

For international matches, the chronometer used must incorporate all the necessary functions (precise timekeeping, a device to time the two-minute expulsion of four players simultaneously and monitor the accumulation of fouls by each team during each period of play).

- 在被要求时，能根据“室内五人制足球竞赛规则诠释和裁判员指南中的‘比赛中选位’和‘比赛停止时选位’（第五章—裁判员）”，在比赛场地上选位。
- 在第三裁判员未到场情况下行使第三裁判员的特殊职责。
- 提供任何与比赛相关的其他信息。

国际比赛

在国际比赛中，必须委派第三裁判员和计时员。

在国际比赛中，计时器须具备所有必需的功能（精确计时、同时记录4名被罚令出场队员2分钟罚停期的计时装置和记录每队各自上下半场的累计犯规次数）。

Periods of play

The match lasts two equal periods of 20 minutes, unless otherwise mutually agreed between the referee and the two teams. Any agreement to alter the duration of the periods of play must be made before the start of play and must comply with the competition rules.

Ending the periods of play

The timekeeper indicates the end of each period with the acoThe timekeeper indicates the end of each 20 minutes period with an acoustic signal or whistle. After hearing the timekeeper' s signal, one of the referees announces the end of the period or match with his whistle, bearing in mind the following:

- If a kick from the second penalty mark or direct free kick, beginning with the sixth accumulated foul, must be taken or retaken, the period in question is extended until the kick has been taken
- If a penalty kick has to be taken or retaken, the period in question is extended until the kick has been taken

If the ball has been played towards one of the goals, before the timekeeper sounds the acoustic signal, the referees must wait for the kick to end before announcing the end of the period of match with a whister The period ends when:

- the ball goes directly into the goal and a goal is scored
- the ball leaves the boundaries of the pitch

比赛半场

比赛分为两个半场，每半场20分钟。特殊情况经裁判员和双方同意另定除外。任何改变比赛时间的决定必须在比赛开始前制定，并要符合竞赛规程。

半场结束

计时员用声音信号或哨声示意每半场结束。在听到计时员的哨声或声音信号后，其中一名裁判员用哨声宣布半场或比赛结束，并要注意下列情况：

- 当需要踢或重踢第二罚球点罚球或第6次累计犯规起的直接任意球时，相关半场应被延长，直到罚球结束。
- 当需踢或重踢球点球时，相关半场应被延长，直到罚球结束。

如果球向其中一个球门运动，裁判员必须在计时员响哨或声音信号之前等踢球结束。半场结束是当：

- 球直接向球门内移动并得分。
- 球离开场地边线。

- the ball touches the goalkeeper or another player in the defending team, the goalposts, crossbar or ground, crosses the goal line and a goal is scored
- the defending goalkeeper or another player in defending team touches the ball or it rebounds from the goalposts or crossbar and does not cross the goal line
- the ball touches any player in the team that played the ball, except if an indirect free kick was taken and the ball was heading towards the opponent's goal after being touched by the second player
- no infringement has been committed that is sanctioned with a direct free kick, an indirect free kick or a penalty kick, and a direct free kick, indirect free kick or penalty kick does not have to be retaken

If an infringement has been committed during this period that is sanctioned with a direct free kick after the fifth accumulated foul of one of the teams, or sanctioned with a penalty kick, the period ends when:

- the ball is not kicked directly at the goal
- the ball goes directly into the goal and a goal is scored
- the ball leaves the boundaries of the pitch
- the ball hits one or both posts, the crossbar, the goalkeeper or anther player in the defending team and a goal is scored
- the ball hits one or both posts, the crossbar, the goalkeeper or another player in the defending team and a goal is not scored
- another infringement sanctioned with a direct free kick, indirect free kick or penalty kick is not committed

- 球触及守门员或防守队员、球门柱、横梁或地面后越过球门线进球得分。
- 守方守门员或队员触及球，或球从球门柱、横梁反弹并未越过球门线。
- 球被任何攻方队员触及，但此球是发出的间接任意球且被另一名球员触及后球向球门移动的情况除外。
- 没有出现可判为直接任意球、间接任意球或球点球的犯规，且不须重踢直接任意球、间接任意球或球点球。

如果在此期间，某队犯有可判为直接任意球的犯规且累计犯规已达5次，或犯有可判为球点球的犯规，半场结束是当：

- 球没有被直接踢向球门。
- 球直接进入球门并得分。
- 球出界。
- 球击中一个或两个门柱、横梁、守方守门员或队员后进门得分。
- 球击中一个或两个门柱、横梁、守方守门员或队员后没有进门。
- 没有出现可判为直接任意球、间接任意球或球点球的另一犯规。

If, during this period, an infringement sanctioned with a direct free kick is committed before the sixth accumulated foul of one of the teams, the period ends when:

- the ball is not kicked directly at the goal
- the ball goes directly into the goal and a goal is scored
- the ball leaves the boundaries of the pitch
- the ball hits one or both posts, the crossbar, the goalkeeper or another player in the defending team and a goal is scored
- the ball hits one or both posts, the crossbar, the goalkeeper or another player in the defending team and a goal is not scored
- the ball touches a player in the team taking the kick
- another infringement sanctioned with a direct free kick, indirect free kick or penalty kick is not committed

If an infringement sanctioned with an indirect free kick is committed during this period, the period ends when:

- the ball goes directly into the goal without being touched by another player during its trajectory or touching one or both of the posts or the crossbar, in which case the goal will not be allowed
- the ball leaves the boundaries of the pitch
- the ball hits one or both posts or the crossbar after touching the goalkeeper or another player in the defending or attacking team, not the team taking the kick, and a goal is scored

如果在此期间，某队犯有可判为直接任意球的犯规但累计犯规次数未达到第6次，半场结束是当：

- 球没有被直接踢向球门。
- 球直接进入球门并得分。
- 球出界。
- 球击中一个或两个门柱、横梁、守方守门员或队员后进门得分。
- 球击中一个或两个门柱、横梁、守方守门员或队员后没有进门。
- 球被攻方队员触及。
- 没有出现可判为直接任意球、间接任意球或球点球的犯规。

如果在此期间，某队犯有可判为间接任意球的犯规，半场结束是当：

- 球在运动中未触及其他球员直接进入球门，或击中一个或两个门柱或横梁后进入球门，此进球无效。
- 球出界。
- 球在触及守门员或非罚球方的其他队员后，击中一个或两个门柱或横梁，且进球得分。

- the ball hits one or both posts or the crossbar after touching the goalkeeper or another player in the defending or attacking team, not the team taking the kick, and a goal is not scored
- no other infringement sanctioned with a direct free kick, indirect free kick or penalty kick is committed

Time-out

The teams are entitled to a one-minute time-out in each period.

The following conditions apply:

- The team officials are authorised to request the third referee, or the timekeeper if there is no third referee, for a one-minute time-out using the document provided
- The timekeeper grants the time-out when the team that has requested it is in possession of the ball and the ball is out of play, using a different whistle or acoustic signal from the ones used by the referees
- During the time-out, the players may remain on or off the pitch. In order to have a drink, the players must leave the pitch
- During the time-out, the substitutes must stay off the pitch
- During the time-out, officials are not allowed to give instructions on the pitch
- Substitutions may only be made after the acoustic signal or whistle has sounded to indicate the end of the time-out

- 球在触及守门员或非罚球方的其他队员后，击中一个或两个门柱或横梁，但未进球得分。
- 没有出现可判为直接任意球、间接任意球或球点球的犯规。

暂停

双方球队在每个半场各有一次1分钟暂停的权利。

应遵循下列条款：

- 球队官员有权向第三裁判员，或在无第三裁判员情况下向计时员使用暂停申请表单提出1分钟暂停申请。
- 当提出暂停请求的球队拥有球权且比赛停止时，计时员用不同于裁判员所使用的哨声或声音信号准予暂停。
- 暂停期间，队员可以留在场上或场外。但如果要喝水，则必须离开比赛场地。
- 暂停期间，替补队员必须保持在场外。
- 暂停期间，官员不允许在场内给予指导。
- 替换队员只有在暂停结束声音信号或哨音响起后进行。

- A team that does not request a time-out in the first half of the match is only entitled to one time-out during the second half
- If there is neither a third referee nor a timekeeper, a team official may request the referees for a time-out
- There are no time-outs during extra time, if played

Half-time interval

Players are entitled to an interval at half-time.

The half-time interval must not exceed 15 minutes.

Competition rules must state the duration of the half-time interval.

The duration of the half-time interval may be altered only with the consent of the referee.

Abandoned match

An abandoned match is replayed unless the competition rules provide otherwise.

- 一队在上半场比赛没有请求暂停，在下半场也只允许请求一次暂停。
- 如果既没有第三裁判员也没有计时员，球队官员可请求裁判员给予暂停。
- 如果进入加时赛，则加时赛期间没有暂停。

中场休息

队员有中场休息的权利。

中场休息不得超过15分钟。

竞赛规程必须注明中场休息的时间。

只有经裁判员同意方可改变中场休息时间。

中止的比赛

除竞赛规程另有规定外，中止的比赛应重新进行。

Preliminaries

A coin is tossed and the team that wins the toss decides which goal it will attack in the first half of the match.

The other team takes the kick-off to start the match.

The team that wins the toss takes the kick-off to start the second half of the match.

In the second half of the match, the teams change ends and attack the opposite goals.

Kick-off

A kick-off is a way of starting or restarting play:

- at the start of the match
- after a goal has been scored
- at the start of the second half of the match
- at the start of each period of extra time, where applicable

A goal may not be scored directly from the kick-off..

Procedure

- All players must be in their own half of the pitch
- The opponents of the team taking the kick-off are at least 3m from the ball until it is in play
- The ball must be stationary on the centre mark
- The referee gives a signal
- The ball is in play when it is kicked and moves forward

预备

通过掷币，猜中的队决定上半场比赛的进攻方向。

另一队开球开始比赛。

猜中的队在下半场开球开始比赛。

下半场比赛，两队交换比赛场地和进攻方向。

开球

开球是比赛开始或重新开始的一种方式：
- 在比赛开始时。
- 在进球得分后。
- 在下半场比赛开始时。
- 在加时赛两个半场开始时。

开球直接进球得分无效。

程序

- 所有队员必须在本方半场内。
- 开球队的对方队员，应距球至少3米，直到比赛开始。
- 球必须放定在中点上。
- 裁判员发出信号。
- 当球被踢并向前移动时比赛即为开始。

After a team scores a goal, provided that the period has not ended, the kick-off is taken by the other team.

Infringements and sanctions

If the ball is in play and the player taking the kick-off touches the ball again (except with his hands) before it has touched another player:

- an indirect free kick is awarded to the opposing team, to be taken from the position of the ball when the infringement occurred (see Law 13 – Position of free kick)

If the ball is in play and the player taking the kick-off deliberately handles the ball before it has touched another player:

- a direct free kick is awarded to the opposing team, to be taken from the position of the ball when the infringement occurred (see Law 13 – Position of free kick) and his team is sanctioned with an accumulated foul

In the event of any other infringement of the kick-off procedure:

- the kick-off is retaken and the advantage cannot be applied

Dropped ball

If, while the ball is still in play, the referees are required to stop play temporarily for any reason not mentioned elsewhere in the Futsal Laws of the Game, the match is restarted with a dropped ball. The match is also restarted with a dropped ball when provided for in the Futsal Laws of the Game.

某队进球得分后，只要该半场还没有结束，由另一队开球。

违规与判罚

如果比赛进行中开球队员在其他队员触球前再次触球（非用手触球）：

- 由对方队在违例发生地点踢间接任意球（参见规则第十三章—任意球的位置）。

如果比赛进行中开球队员在其他队员触球前故意手球：

- 由对方队在违例发生地点踢直接任意球（参见规则第十三章—任意球的位置)，并记录该队累计犯规。

在开球程序上的其他任何犯规：

- 重新开球且不适用有利条款。

坠球

如果在比赛进行中，裁判员因室内五人制足球竞赛规则未提到的任何原因而需要暂停比赛，则以坠球重新开始比赛。在室内五人制足球竞赛规则范围内也可以用坠球的方式重新开始比赛。

Procedure

The referee or second referee drops the ball from the position of the ball when play was stopped, unless play was stopped inside the penalty area, in which case one of the referees drops the ball on the penalty area line at the point nearest to where the ball was located when play was stopped.

Play restarts when the ball touches the ground within the boundaries of the pitch. If the ball leaves the pitch after it makes contact with the ground, without a player touching it after being in play, the ball is dropped at the same point where it was dropped the first time.

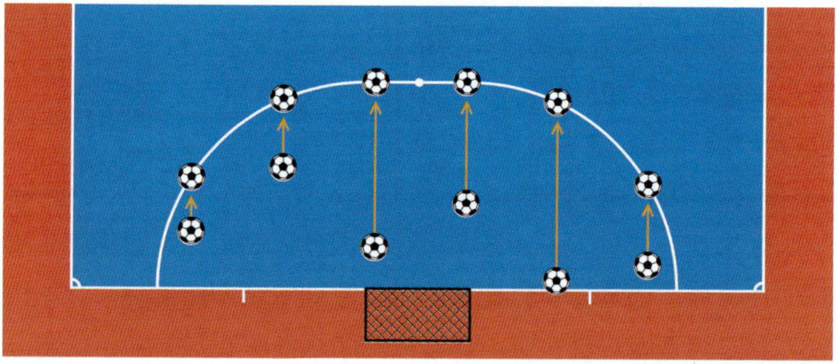

程序

裁判员或第二裁判员在比赛停止时球所在地点坠球，除非比赛在罚球区内被停止。在这种情况下，其中一名裁判员在比赛停止时距球所处地点最近的罚球区线上坠球。

当球在比赛场地内触地比赛即重新开始。如果球触及地面，比赛进行后未触及任一队员离开场地，则在最初坠球的地点重新坠球。

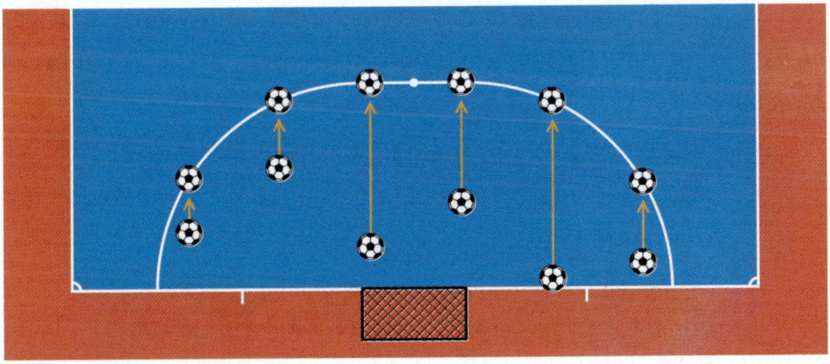

Infringements and sanctions

The ball is dropped again at the same place where it was dropped the first time:

- if it is touched by a player before it makes contact with the ground
- if the ball leaves the pitch after it makes contact with the ground without a player touching it
- if any infringement is committed before the ball makes contact with the ground

If, after the ball has made contact with the ground, a player kicks it once directly towards one of the goals and the ball goes directly:

- into the opponent's goal, a goal clearance is awarded
- into the team's own goal, a corner kick is awarded to the opposing team

If, after the ball has made contact with the ground, a player kicks the ball with more than one touch towards one of the goals and:

- the ball enters one of the goals, a goal is awarded

违规与判罚

在最初坠球的地点重新坠球：

- 如果球在接触地面前被队员触及。
- 如果球在接触地面后未经任何队员触及出界。
- 如果在球触及地面前有任何犯规发生。

如果在球接触地面后，一名队员直接将球踢向某一球门，并且：

- 球进入对方球门，由对方掷球门球。
- 球进入本方球门，由对方踢角球。

如果在球接触地面后，一名队员通过多次触球将球踢向某一球门，并且：

- 球进入某一球门，进球有效。

Ball out of play

The ball is out of play when:

- it has wholly crossed the goal line or touch line whether on the ground or in the air
- play has been stopped by the referees
- it hits the ceiling

Ball in play

The ball is in play at all other times, including when:

- it rebounds off a goalpost or crossbar and remains on the pitch
- it rebounds off the referees when they are on the pitch

Indoor pitch

The minimum height of ceilings is 4m and shall be stipulated in the competition rules.

If the ball hits the ceiling while in play, the game is restarted with a kick-in taken by the opponents of the team that last touched the ball. The kick-in is taken from the point on the touch line nearest to the place on the ground above which the ball hit the ceiling (see Law 15 – Position of kick-in).

比赛停止

下列情形比赛停止：

- 当球的整体从空中或地面越过球门线或边线时。
- 当比赛被裁判员停止时。
- 当球击打到天花板时。

比赛进行

其他所有时间比赛都视为进行中，包括下列情形：

- 球从球门柱或横梁弹回球场内。
- 球从场内的裁判员身上反弹回场内。

室内球场

天花板最低高度为4米且由竞赛规程规定。

在室内球场比赛时，如球意外击中天花板，则由最后触球队员的对方队，以踢界外球的方式重新开始比赛。此界外球应在距球触天花板垂直下方最近的边线处踢出（参见规则第十五章—踢界外球的位置）。

Goal scored

A goal is scored when the whole of the ball passes over the goal line, between the goalposts and under the crossbar, provided that no infringement of the Futsal Laws of the Game has been committed previously by the team scoring the goal.

A goal is disallowed if the goalkeeper of the attacking team throws or hits the ball intentionally with his hand or arm from inside his own penalty area and is the last player to touch or play the ball. The match is restarted with a goal clearance to the opposing team.

If, after a goal is scored, the referees realise, before play restarts, that the team that scored the goal was playing with an extra player or hasd carried out a substitution incorrectly, they must disallow the goal and restart play with an indirect free kick to be taken by the opponents of the offending player from any point inside the penalty area. If the kick-off has already been taken, they section the offending player in accordance with Law 3, but the goal is allowed. The referees report the fact to the appropriate authorities. If the goal was scored by the other team, they must allow it.

Winning team

The team scoring the greater number of goals during a match is the winner. If both teams score an equal number of goals, or if no goals are scored, the match is drawn.

进球得分

当球的整体从球门柱间及横梁下越过球门线，而此前进球的球队未违反室内五人制足球竞赛规则，即为进球得分。

如果攻方守门员故意用手或上臂从本方罚球区内将球掷或打入对方球门，并且他是最后触及或击球的队员，则进球无效。比赛将由对方球队掷球门球重新开始比赛。

如果进球后，裁判员在比赛重新开始前意识到进球队多出1人或已经进行了不正确换人，则应宣布进球无效并由对方球队从罚球区内的任何地点以间接任意球重新开始比赛。如果已经开球，裁判员依据竞赛规则第三章采取措施处罚攻方队员，但进球有效。裁判员应向相应的主办机构报告相关事实。如果另一队进球，则进球有效。

获胜球队

在比赛中进球数多的队为胜者。如果两队进球数相等或均未进球，则比赛为平局。

Competition rules

When the competition rules require there to be a winning team after a match or home-and-away tie, the following are the only permitted procedures for determining the winning team:

- away goals rule
- extra time
- kicks from the penalty mark

These procedures are described in the section entitled "Procedures to Determine the Winner of a Match or Home-and-Away Tie".

竞赛规程

当一场比赛或主客场两回合比赛成平局，而竞赛规程需要决出胜者时，仅允许以下列程序决定胜队：

- 客场进球规则。
- 加时赛。
- 踢球点球。

这些步骤在本规则“决定一场或主客场比赛胜负的程序”章节中。

There is no offside in futsal.

室内五人制足球没有越位。

Fouls and misconduct are infringements of the Futsal Laws of the Game that are penalised as follows:

Fouls

Fouls are penalised with a direct free kick, penalty kick or indirect free kick.

Fouls penalised with a direct free kick

A direct free kick is awarded to the opposing team if a player commits any of the following seven offences in a manner considered by the referees to be careless, reckless or using excessive force:

- Kicks or attempts to kick an opponent
- Trips an opponent
- Jumps at an opponent
- Charges an opponent
- Strikes or attempts to strike an opponent
- Pushes an opponent
- Tackles an opponent

A direct free kick is also awarded to the opposing team if a player commits any of the following three offences:

- Holds an opponent
- Spits at an opponent
- Handles the ball deliberately (except for the goalkeeper within his own penalty area)

下列行为违反了室内五人制足球竞赛规则，将被罚犯规或不正当行为：

犯规

犯规将被判罚直接任意球、罚球点球或间接任意球。

判为直接任意球的犯规

如果裁判员认为，队员以草率地、鲁莽地或使用过分力量的方式犯有下列7种犯规中的任何一种，将判给对方踢直接任意球：

- 踢或企图踢对方队员。
- 绊摔对方队员。
- 跳向对方队员。
- 冲撞对方队员。
- 打或企图打对方队员。
- 推对方队员。
- 抢截对方队员。

如果队员犯有下列3种犯规中的任何一种，也判给对方踢直接任意球：

- 阻止对方队员移动。
- 向对方队员吐唾沫。
- 故意手球（守门员在本方罚球区内除外）。

A direct free kick is taken from the place where the offence occurred (see Law 13 – Position of free kick).

The above offences are accumulated fouls.

Fouls penalised with a penalty kick

A penalty kick is awarded if any of the above ten offences is committed by a player inside his own penalty area, irrespective of the position of the ball, provided it is in play.

在犯规发生地点踢直接任意球（参见规则第十三章—任意球的位置）。

上述犯规都属于累计犯规之列。

判为罚球点球的犯规

在比赛进行中，无论球在什么位置，如果队员在本方罚球区内违反了上述10种犯规中的任何一种，应被判罚球点球。

Fouls penalised with an indirect free kick

An indirect free kick is awarded to the opposing team if a goalkeeper commits any of the following four offences:

- Controls the ball with his hands or feet in his own half of the pitch for more than four seconds
- After playing the ball, he touches it again in his own half of the pitch after it has been deliberately played to him by a team-mate without an opponent playing or touching it
- Touches the ball with his hands inside his own penalty area after it has been deliberately kicked to him by a team-mate
- Touches the ball with his hands inside his own penalty area after he has received it directly from a kick-in by a team-mate

An indirect free kick is also awarded to the opposing team if, in the opinion of the referees, a player:

- plays in a dangerous manner in the presence of an opponent
- impedes the progress of an opponent
- prevents the goalkeeper from releasing the ball from his hands
- commits against a team-mate one of the nine offences penalised with a direct free kick if they are committed against an opponent
- commits any other infringement not previously mentioned in Law 12 or in any other Law, for which play is stopped to caution or dismiss a player

The indirect free kick is taken from the place where the offence occurred (see Law 13 – Position of free kick).

判为间接任意球的犯规

如果守门员犯有下列4种犯规中的任何一种，判由对方踢间接任意球：

- 在本方半场内，以手或脚控制球超过4秒。
- 将球传出后，未经对方队员踢或触及在本方半场内再次触及同队队员故意传给他的球。
- 在本方罚球区内，以手触及同队队员故意踢给他的球。
- 在本方罚球区内，以手触及同队队员直接踢给他的界外球。

如果裁判员认为队员犯有下列犯规中的任何一种，则也判由对方在犯规地点踢间接任意球：

- 在对方队员面前以危险方式比赛。
- 阻挡对方行进路线。
- 阻挡对方守门员将球从手中发出。
- 采用可判为直接任意球的9种犯规之一的行为对本方队员犯规。
- 犯有竞赛规则第十二章或其他章节未提及的任何其他犯规，裁判员为此停止比赛对犯规队员进行警告或罚令出场。

在犯规发生地点踢间接任意球（参见规则第十三章—任意球的位置）。

Misconduct

Misconduct is penalised with a caution or a sending-off.

Disciplinary sanctions

The yellow card is used to communicate that a player or substitute has been cautioned.

The red card is used to communicate that a player or substitute has been sent off.

Only a player or substitute may be shown the red or yellow card. The relevant card is shown publicly and only on the pitch if the match has started. In other cases, the referees verbally inform the players and team officials of the disciplinary sanction taken.

The referees have the authority to take disciplinary sanctions from the moment they enter the premises where the pitch is located before the start of the match until they leave them.

A player who commits a cautionable or sending-off offence, either on or off the pitch, whether directed towards an opponent, a team-mate, the referees or any other person, is disciplined according to the nature of the offence committed.

不正当行为

不正当行为将被警告或罚令出场。

纪律制裁

黄牌用于表示对一名队员或替补队员的警告。

红牌用于表示将一名队员或替补队员罚令出场。

黄牌和红牌只能出示给队员和替补队员。一旦比赛开始，相关的红黄牌应公开出示以及仅限于在比赛场地上。在其他情况下，裁判员口头告知队员和球队官员对其的纪律制裁。

赛前进入赛场直到离开，均有权对队员进行纪律处罚。

队员无论是在比赛场内或场外，无论是直接对对方队员、同队队员、裁判员或任何其他人犯有应被警告或罚令出场的行为，都将根据犯规性质进行处罚。

Cautionable offences

A player is cautioned if he commits any of the following seven offences:

- Unsporting behaviour
- Dissent by word or action
- Persistent infringement of the Futsal Laws of the Game
- Delaying the restart of play
- Failure to respect the required distance when play is restarted with a corner kick, free kick or kick-in (defending players)
- Entering or re-entering the pitch without the referees' permission or in contravention of the substitution procedure
- Deliberately leaving the pitch without the referees' permission

A substitute is cautioned if he commits any of the following four infringements:

- Unsporting behaviour
- Dissent by word or action
- Delaying the restart of play
- Entering the pitch in contravention of the substitution procedure

可警告的犯规

如果队员犯有下列7种犯规中的任何一种，将被警告：

- 非体育行为。
- 用语言或行动表示异议。
- 持续违反室内五人制足球竞赛规则。
- 延误比赛重新开始。
- 当以角球、任意球或踢界外球重新开始比赛时（防守队员），不退出规定的距离。
- 未经裁判员许可进入或重新进入比赛场地，或违反替换程序。
- 未经裁判员许可故意离开比赛场地。

如果替补队员犯有下列4种犯规中的任何一种，将被警告：

- 非体育行为。
- 用语言或行动表示异议。
- 延误比赛重新开始。
- 进入比赛场地时违反替换程序。

Sending-off offences

A player or substitute is sent off if he commits any of the following seven offences:

- Serious foul play
- Violent conduct
- Spitting at an opponent or any other person
- Denying the opposing team a goal or an obvious goalscoring opportunity by deliberately handling the ball (this does not apply to a goalkeeper within his own penalty area)
- Denying an obvious goalscoring opportunity to an opponent moving towards the player's goal by an offence punishable by a free kick or a penalty kick
- Using offensive, insulting or abusive language and/or gestures
- Receiving a second caution in the same match

A substitute is sent off if he commits the following offence:

- Denying a goal or an obvious goalscoring opportunity

A player or substitute who has been sent off must leave the vicinity of the pitch and the technical area.

罚令出场的犯规

如果队员或替补队员犯有下列7种犯规中的任何一种，将被罚令出场：

- 严重犯规。
- 暴力行为。
- 向对方或其他任何人吐唾沫。
- 用故意手球破坏对方的进球或明显的进球得分机会（不包括守门员在本方罚球区内）。

- 用可判为任意球或球点球的犯规，破坏对方向本方球门移动着的明显进球得分机会。
- 使用攻击性、侮辱性或辱骂性的语言或手势。
- 在同一场比赛中得到第二次警告。

如果替补队员犯有下列犯规，将被罚令出场：

- 破坏对方的进球或明显的进球得分机会。

被罚令出场的队员或替补队员必须离开比赛场地附近和技术区域。

Types of free kick

Free kicks are either direct or indirect.

The direct free kick

Signal

One of the referees signals the direct free kick by keeping one arm horizontal and pointing in the direction the kick has to be taken. The referee points to the ground with his other hand to make it plain to the third referee and the timekeeper that it is an accumulated foul.

Ball enters the goal

- If a direct free kick is kicked directly into the opponents' goal, a goal is awarded
- If a direct free kick is kicked directly into the team's own goal, a corner kick is awarded to the opposing team

任意球类型

任意球分为直接任意球和间接任意球。

直接任意球

信号

裁判员单臂平举，指向发球方向。裁判员另一手指向地面，以向第三裁判员和计时员示意，此为累计犯规。

球进球门

- 如果直接任意球直接踢入对方球门，判为得分。
- 如果直接任意球直接踢入本方球门，判给对方踢角球。

Accumulated fouls

- Accumulated fouls are those penalised with a direct free kick or penalty kick mentioned in Law 12
- The accumulated fouls committed by each team in each period are recorded in the match report
- The referees may allow play to continue by applying the advantage if the team has not previously committed five accumulated fouls and the opposing team is not denied a goal or an obvious goalscoring opportunity
- If they apply the advantage, the referees use the mandatory signals to indicate an accumulated foul to the timekeeper and third referee as soon as the ball is out of play
- If extra time is played, accumulated fouls from the second period continue to accumulate during extra time

累计犯规

- 是指第十二章中提到的应判罚直接任意球或罚球点球的犯规。
- 每队在每半场的累计犯规应被记录在比赛报告中。
- 如果某队犯规尚未累计到5次，且对方队也未因此失去进球或明显进球得分机会，裁判员可以掌握有利让比赛继续进行。
- 如果裁判员掌握有利，当比赛停止时，必须用规定的信号向计时员及第三裁判员示意累计犯规。
- 如果有加时赛，加时赛中的累计犯规应继续累计在下半场累计犯规次数上。

The indirect free kick

Signal

The referees indicate an indirect free kick by raising their arms above their heads. They maintain their arms in that position until the kick has been taken and the ball has touched another player or goes out of play.

Ball enters the goal

A goal can be scored only if the ball subsequently touches another player before it enters the goal:

- If an indirect free kick is kicked directly into the opponents' goal, a goal clearance is awarded
- If an indirect free kick is kicked directly into the team's own goal, a corner kick is awarded to the opposing team

Procedure

For both direct and indirect free kicks, the ball must be stationary when the kick is taken.

Direct free kick beginning with the sixth accumulated foul by each team

- The player taking the free kick kicks the ball with the intention of scoring a goal and may not pass the ball to a team-mate

间接任意球

信号

当裁判员判罚间接任意球时，应单臂上举过头，并保持这种姿势直到球踢出后被其他队员触及或比赛停止。

球进球门

只有当球进门前触及到另一名队员才算得分有效：

- 如果间接任意球直接踢入对方球门，判给对方掷球门球。
- 如果间接任意球直接踢入本方球门，判给对方踢角球。

程序

无论是直接任意球还是间接任意球，踢球时必须将球放定。

每队从第6次累计犯规起的直接任意球：

- 任意球必须直接射门而不能传给同队队员。

- Once the free kick has been taken, no player may touch the ball until it has been touched by the defending goalkeeper, rebounded off one of the goalposts or the crossbar, or left the pitch
- If a player commits his team's sixth accumulated foul in the opposing team's half or in his own half in the area bordered by the halfway line and an imaginary line parallel to the halfway line passing through the second penalty mark, the free kick is taken from the second penalty mark. The location of the second penalty mark is indicated in Law 1. The free kick is taken in accordance with the section entitled "Position of free kick"
- If a player commits his team's sixth accumulated foul in his own half of the pitch between the imaginary 10m line and the goal line but outside the penalty area, the attacking team decides whether to take it from the second penalty mark or the place where the infringement occurred
- Beginning with the sixth accumulated foul, additional time is allowed to take a direct free kick at the end of each half or at the end of each period of extra time

Position of free kick

Free kick outside the penalty area

- All opponents must be at least 5m from the ball until it is in play

- 任意球踢出后，只有球被守方守门员触及，或从球门柱、横梁弹回，或球出界后，其他队员才可触球。
- 如果队员出现本方的第6次累计犯规，而犯规地点在对方半场或本方半场介于通过第二罚球点的假想平行线与中线之间的区域，该任意球在犯规方半场的第二罚球点踢出，其程序须遵循本章“任意球的位置”要求。第二罚球点的位置已在第一章中说明。
- 如果队员出现本方的第6次累计犯规，而犯规地点在犯规方半场球门线和通过10米的假想平行线之间、罚球区之外的区域，则对方可选择在犯规地点或第二罚球点踢任意球。
- 在每半场比赛或加时赛上下半场结束时，应允许延长时间执行完自第6次累计犯规起的直接任意球。

任意球的位置

罚球区外的任意球

- 所有对方队员必须距球至少5米直到比赛进行。

- The ball is in play when it is kicked and moves
- The free kick is taken from the place where the infringement occurred or from the position of the ball when the infringement occurred (according to the infringement) or from the second penalty mark

Direct or indirect free kick inside the penalty area to the defending team

- All opponents must be at least 5m from the ball until it is in play
- All opponents must remain outside the penalty area until the ball is in play
- The ball is in play when it is kicked directly out of the penalty area
- A free kick awarded in the penalty area may be taken from any point inside that area

- 当球被踢并移动时比赛即为进行。
- 在犯规发生地点，或在犯规发生时比赛球所在的地点（根据犯规情况），或从第二罚球点踢任意球。

在守方罚球区内的直接或间接任意球

- 所有对方队员必须距球至少5米直到比赛进行。
- 所有对方队员必须位于罚球区外直到比赛进行。
- 当球被直接踢出罚球区比赛即为进行。
- 在罚球区内获得的任意球可以在罚球区内任何地点执行。

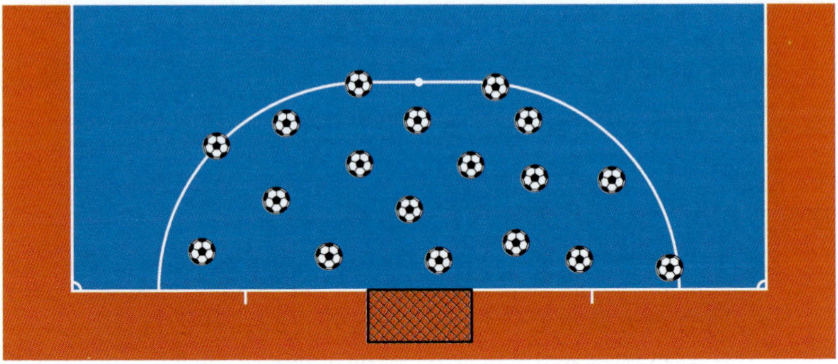

Direct free kick beginning with the sixth accumulated foul in each period

- The defending team's players may not form a wall to defend free kicks
- The player taking the kick is properly identified
- The goalkeeper remains in his penalty area at a distance of at least 5m from the ball
- The players remain on the pitch, except the kicker if he wishes
- The players, except the kicker and the defending goalkeeper, remain behind an imaginary line that is level with the ball and parallel to the goal line and outside the penalty area, at a distance of 5m from the ball. They may not obstruct the player taking the free kick. No player, except the kicker, may cross this imaginary line until the ball is in play

Indirect free kick for the attacking team

- All opponents must be at least 5m from the ball until it is in play
- The ball is in play when it is kicked and moves
- An indirect free kick conceded in the penalty area is taken from the penalty area line at the point nearest to where the offence was committed

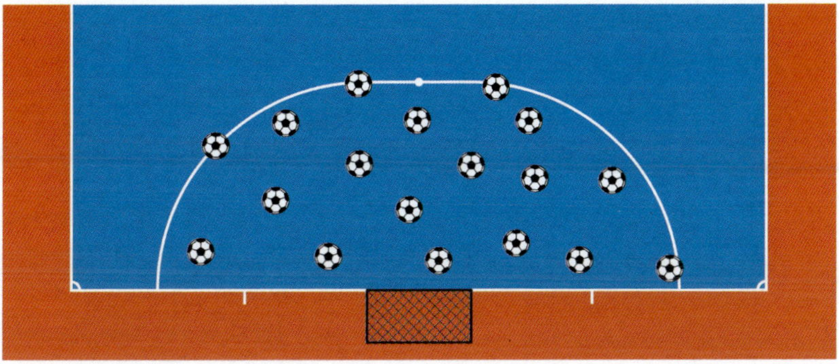

每半场累计第6次犯规起的直接任意球

- 守方队不可排人墙防守。
- 须明确主罚队员。
- 守方守门员须留在罚球区内且距球至少5米。
- 队员须留在场地内，主罚队员可选择从场外开始助跑。
- 除主罚队员和守方守门员外，其他队员应在与球齐平而且平行于球门线的一条假想线后、罚球区外，并且至少距球5米，不可阻挡主罚队员。除主罚队员外，其他队员直到比赛进行方可越过假想线。

进攻队间接任意球

- 所有对方队员必须距球至少5米直到比赛进行。
- 当球被踢并移动时，比赛即为开始。
- 在罚球区内的间接任意球，应从距犯规发生地点最近的罚球区线上踢出。

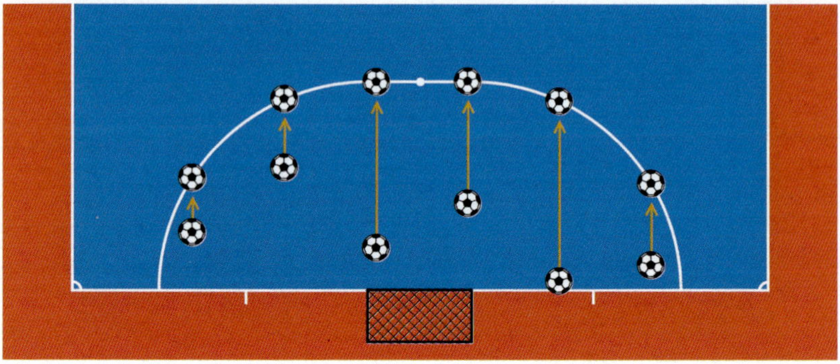

Infringements and sanctions

If, when a free kick is taken, an opponent is closer to the ball than the required distance:

- the kick is retaken and the offending player is cautioned, unless the advantage can be applied or another infringement is committed that is punishable by a penalty kick. If the infringement is punishable by a free kick, the referees decide whether to punish the original infringement or the one committed subsequently. If the second infringement is punishable by a penalty kick or direct free kick, an accumulated foul is recorded against the offending team

If, when a free kick is taken by the defending team from inside its own penalty area, the ball is not kicked directly out of the penalty area:

- the kick is retaken

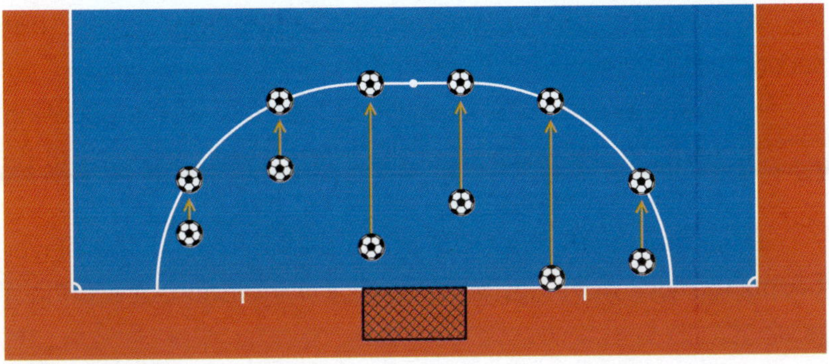

违规与判罚

如果当任意球踢出时，对方队员比规定距离更接近于球：

- 任意球应重踢并警告犯规队员，除非裁判员掌握有利或者有其他可判为罚球点球的犯规发生。如果该犯规可被判为任意球，则由裁判员决定是判罚该犯规还是判罚原来的犯规。如果该犯规可判为罚球点球或直接任意球，防守一方应累计1次犯规。

如果从本方罚球区内踢任意球，球未直接踢出罚球区：

- 任意球重踢。

If the team taking the free kick takes more than four seconds:

- the referees award an indirect free kick to the opposing team, to be taken from the place where play was to be restarted (see Law 13 – Position of free kick)

Beginning with the sixth accumulated foul, if the player taking the kick does not do so with the intention of scoring a goal:

- the referees award an indirect free kick to the opposing team, to be taken from the place where play was to be restarted

Beginning with the sixth accumulated foul, if a free kick is taken by a team-mate of the player who had been identified previously:

- the referees stop play, caution him for unsporting behaviour and restart the match with an indirect free kick to the defending team to be taken from where he kicked the ball

Free kick taken by a player other than the goalkeeper

If, after the ball is in play, the kicker touches the ball again (except with his hands) before it has touched another player:

- an indirect free kick is awarded to the opposing team, to be taken from the place where the infringement occurred (see Law 13 – Position of free kick)

如果某队踢任意球超过4秒时：

- 裁判员判给其对方队踢间接任意球，并在原地点执行（参见规则第十三章—任意球的位置）。

从第6次累计犯规开始，如果队员罚球时没有射门得分的意图：

- 裁判员判给其对方队踢间接任意球，并在原地点执行。

从第6次累计犯规开始，如果由事先确定的主罚队员的队友来踢任意球：

- 裁判员停止比赛，警告其非体育行为，由防守方在其踢球的地点踢间接任意球重新开始比赛。

由守门员外的队员踢任意球

如果比赛进行后，主罚队员在其他队员触球前再次触及球（用手除外）：

- 判由对方在犯规发生地点踢间接任意球（参见规则第十三章—任意球的位置）。

If, after the ball is in play, the kicker deliberately handles the ball before it has touched another player:

- a direct free kick is awarded to the opposing team, to be taken from the place where the infringement occurred (see Law 13 – Position of free kick), and his team is sanctioned with an accumulated foul
- a penalty kick is awarded if the infringement was committed inside the kicker's penalty area, and his team is sanctioned with an accumulated foul

Free kick taken by the goalkeeper

If, after the ball is in play, the goalkeeper touches the ball again (except with his hands), before it has touched another player:

- an indirect free kick is awarded to the opposing team, to be taken from the place where the infringement occurred (see Law 13 – Position of free kick)

If, after the ball is in play, the goalkeeper deliberately handles the ball before it has touched another player:

- a direct free kick is awarded to the opposing team if the infringement occurred outside the goalkeeper's penalty area, to be taken from the place where the infringement occurred (see Law 13 – Position of free kick) and his team is sanctioned with an accumulated foul
- an indirect free kick is awarded to the opposing team if the infringement occurred inside the goalkeeper's penalty area, to be taken from the place where the infringement occurred (see Law 13 – Position of free kick)

如果比赛进行后，主罚队员在其他队员触球前故意手球：

- 判由对方在犯规发生地点踢直接任意球（参见规则第十三章—任意球的位置），并记录该队1次累计犯规。
- 如果犯规发生地点在踢球队员本方罚球区内，将判罚球点球，并记录该队1次累计犯规。

守门员罚任意球

如果比赛进行后，守门员在其他队员触球前再次触及球（用手除外）：

- 判由对方在犯规发生地点踢间接任意球（参见规则第十三章—任意球的位置）。

如果比赛进行后，守门员在其他队员触球前故意手球：

- 守门员在本方罚球区外，判由对方在犯规发生地点踢直接任意球（参见规则第十三章—任意球的位置），并记录该队1次累计犯规。
- 守门员在本方罚球区内，判由对方在犯规发生地点踢间接任意球（参见规则第十三章—任意球的位置）。

If the referees give the signal to take the direct free kick, beginning with the sixth accumulated foul, and before the ball is in play:

a player of the team taking the kick infringes the Futsal Laws of the Game, except if the kicker takes longer than four seconds:

- the referees allow the kick to be taken
- if the ball enters the goal, the kick is retaken
- if the ball does not enter the goal, the referees stop play and order the match to be restarted with an indirect free kick to the defending team, to be taken from the place where the infringement occurred (see Law 13 – Position of free kick)

a player of the defending team infringes the Futsal Laws of the Game:

- the referees allow the kick to be taken
- if the ball enters the goal, a goal is awarded
- if the ball does not enter the goal, the kick is retaken

one or more players of the defending team and one or more players of the attacking team infringe the Futsal Laws of the Game:

- the kick is retaken

从第6次累计犯规开始，如果裁判员鸣哨给出罚直接任意球的信号后，球未被踢出之前：

一名攻方队员违反室内五人制足球竞赛规则，除主罚队员用时超过4秒之外：

- 裁判员允许球被踢出。
- 如果球进入球门，则判重踢任意球。
- 如果球未进入球门，裁判员停止比赛并判由守方球队在犯规发生地点踢间接任意球重新开始比赛（参见规则第十三章—任意球的位置）。

一名守方队员违反室内五人制足球竞赛规则：

- 裁判员允许球被踢出。
- 如果球进入球门，则判进球有效。
- 如果球未进入球门，则判重踢任意球。

一名或多名守方队员和一名或多名攻方队员均违反室内五人制足球竞赛规则：

- 判重踢任意球。

Beginning with the sixth accumulated foul, if, after the direct free kick has been taken:

the kicker does not kick the ball forward with the intention of scoring a goal:

- the referees stop play and order the match to be restarted with an indirect free kick to the defending team, to be taken from the place where the offence occurred (see Law 13 – Position of free kick)

the kicker touches the ball again (except with his hands) before it has touched another player:

- an indirect free kick is awarded to the opposing team, to be taken from the place where the infringement occurred (see Law 13 – Position of free kick)

a different player from the kicker touches the ball (except with his hands) before it has touched the defending goalkeeper, rebounded off one of the goalposts or the crossbar or left the pitch:

- an indirect free kick is awarded to the opposing team, to be taken from the place where the infringement occurred (see Law 13 – Position of free kick)

从第6次累计犯规开始，如果直接任意球已经被踢出：

主罚队员没有射门得分的意图：

- 则裁判员停止比赛，判由对方在犯规发生地点踢间接任意球重新开始比赛（参见规则第十三章—任意球的位置）。

主罚队员在其他队员触球前再次触球（用手除外）：

- 判由对方在犯规发生地点踢间接任意球（参见规则第十三章—任意球的位置）。

一名非主罚队员在球触及守方守门员，或从任一球门柱或横梁反弹，或离开比赛场地前触及球（用手除外）：

- 判由对方在犯规发生地点踢间接任意球（参见规则第十三章—任意球的位置）。

a player deliberately handles the ball:

- a direct free kick is awarded to the opposing team, to be taken from the place where the infringement occurred (see Law 13 – Position of free kick) and his team is sanctioned with an accumulated foul
- a penalty kick is awarded if the infringement was committed by a player from the defending team inside his own penalty area, except for the defending goalkeeper (see Law 13 – Position of free kick) and his team is sanctioned with an accumulated foul

the ball is touched by an outside agent as it moves forward:

- the kick is retaken

the ball rebounds on to the pitch from the goalkeeper, the crossbar or the goalposts, and is then touched by an outside agent:

- the referees stop play
- play is restarted with a dropped ball at the place where it touched the outside agent, unless it touched the outside agent inside the penalty area, in which case one of the referees drops the ball on the penalty area line at the point nearest to where the ball was located when play was stopped

the ball bursts or becomes defective while in play and has not previously touched the goalposts, the crossbar or another player:

- the kick is retaken

一名队员故意手球：

- 判由对方在犯规发生地点踢直接任意球（参见规则第十三章—任意球的位置），并记录该队1次累计犯规。
- 如果犯规发生地点在守方队员罚球区内，守方守门员除外（参见规则第十三章—任意球的位置），将判罚球点球，并记录该队1次累计犯规。

球向前移动时被场外因素触及：

- 判重踢任意球。

球从守门员、球门柱、横梁反弹回场地内并被场外因素触及：

- 裁判员停止比赛。
- 在球触及场外因素的地点坠球重新开始比赛。除非球触及场外因素的地点在罚球区内，在这种情况下则由其中一名裁判员在比赛停止时距球处地点最近的罚球区线上坠球重新开始比赛。

在比赛进行后，球在没有触及球门柱、横梁或其他队员之前破裂或出现破损：

- 判重踢任意球。

A penalty kick is awarded against a team that commits any of the ten offences for which a direct free kick is awarded, inside its own penalty area and while the ball is in play.

A goal may be scored directly from a penalty kick.

Additional time is allowed for a penalty kick to be taken at the end of each half or at the end of each period of extra time.

Position of the ball and the players

The ball:

- must be placed on the penalty mark

The player taking the penalty kick:

- must be properly identified

The defending goalkeeper:

- must remain on his goal line, facing the kicker, between the goalposts until the ball has been kicked

The players other than the kicker must be located:

- on the pitch
- outside the penalty area
- behind the penalty mark
- at least 5m from the penalty mark

当比赛进行中，一队员在本方罚球区内犯有任何可判为直接任意球的10种犯规，应被判罚球点球。

罚球点球直接进球得分有效。

在每半场比赛或加时赛上下半场结束时，应允许延长时间执行完罚球点球。

球和队员的位置

球：

- 必须放在罚球点上。

主罚球点球的队员：

- 必须明确主罚队员。

防守方的守门员：

- 必须位于本方两球门柱之间的球门线上，面向主罚队员直至球被踢出。

除主罚队员外的其他队员应处于：

- 比赛场地内。
- 罚球区外。
- 罚球点后。
- 距罚球点至少5米。

Procedure

- After the players have taken positions in accordance with this Law, one of the referees signals for the penalty kick to be taken
- The player taking the penalty kick must kick the ball forward
- The ball is in play when it is kicked and moves forward

When a penalty kick is taken during the normal course of play, or time has been extended at half-time or full time or at the end of a period of extra time, if any, to allow a penalty kick to be taken or retaken, a goal is awarded if, before passing between the goalposts and under the crossbar:

- the ball touches either or both goalposts and/or the crossbar and/or the goalkeeper

The referees decide when a penalty kick has been completed.

Infringements and sanctions

If the player taking the penalty kick does not kick the ball forward:

- the referees stop play and order the match to be restarted with an indirect free kick to the defending team, to be taken from the penalty mark (see Law 13 – Position of free kick)

程序

- 在队员按照规则要求处于规定的位置后，其中的一名裁判员发出执行罚球点球的信号。
- 主罚队员必须将球向前踢出。
- 当球被踢并向前移动时比赛即为进行。

在比赛进行中，以及在上半场、全场或加时赛结束而延长时间执行或重新执行罚球点球时，如果球在越过球门柱之间和横梁下的球门线之前遇到下列情况，应判定得分：

- 当球触及一个或两个门柱或横梁或守门员。

裁判员决定罚球点球何时结束。

违规与判罚

如果主罚队员没有将球向前踢出：

- 裁判员停止比赛，由守方在罚球点上踢间接任意球重新开始比赛（参见规则第十三章—任意球的位置）。

If, while a penalty kick is being taken, the ball is kicked by a team-mate of the player who had been previously identified:

- the referees stop play, caution him for unsporting behaviour and order the match to be restarted with an indirect free kick to the defending team, to be taken from the penalty mark (see Law 13 – Position of free kick)

If the referees give the signal for the penalty kick to be taken and, before the ball is in play, one of the following occurs:

a player of the same team as the player taking the kick infringes the Futsal Laws of the Game:

- the referees allow the kick to be taken
- if the ball enters the goal, the kick is retaken
- if the ball does not enter the goal, the referees stop play and order the match to be restarted with an indirect free kick to the defending team, to be taken from the place where the offence occurred (see Law 13 – Position of free kick)

a player of the defending team infringes the Futsal Laws of the Game:

- the referees allow the kick to be taken
- if the ball enters the goal, a goal is awarded
- if the ball does not enter the goal, the kick is retaken

one or more players of the defending team and one or more players of the attacking team infringe the Futsal Laws of the Game:

- the kick is retaken

如果在罚球点球过程中，球被先前确认为主罚队员的队友踢出：

- 裁判员停止比赛，警告其非体育行为，由守方在罚球点上踢间接任意球重新开始比赛（参见规则第十三章—任意球的位置）。

如果裁判员发出执行罚球点球信号后，球进入比赛前发生下列情况：

主罚队员的同队队员违反室内五人制足球竞赛规则：

- 裁判员允许踢出该球点球。
- 如果球进入球门，应重踢。
- 如果球未进入球门，裁判员应停止比赛，由守方在违规地点踢间接任意球重新开始比赛（参见规则第十三章—任意球的位置）。

一名防守方队员违反室内五人制足球竞赛规则：

- 裁判员允许该球点球踢出。
- 如果球进入球门，进球有效。
- 如果球未进入球门，应重踢。

一名或多名守方队员和一名或多名攻方队员均违反室内五人制足球竞赛规则：

- 应重踢。

If, after the penalty kick has been taken:

the kicker touches the ball again (except with his hands) befthe kicker touches the ball again (except with his hands) before it has touched another player:

- an indirect free kick is awarded to the opposing team, to be taken from the place where the infringement occurred (see Law 13 – Position of free kick)

the kicker deliberately handles the ball before it has touched another player:

- a direct free kick is awarded to the opposing team, to be taken from the place where the infringement occurred (see Law 13 – Position of free kick) and his team is sanctioned with an accumulated foul

the ball is touched by an outside agent as it moves forward:

- the kick is retaken

the ball rebounds on to the pitch from the goalkeeper, the crossbar or the goalposts, and is then touched by an outside agent:

- the referees stop play
- play is restarted with a dropped ball at the place where it touched the outside agent, unless it touched the outside agent inside the penalty area, in which case one of the referees drops the ball on the penalty area line at the point nearest to where the ball was located when play was stopped

the ball bursts or becomes defective when in play and has not previously touched the goalposts, the crossbar or a player:

- the kick is retaken

如果罚球点球踢出后：

主罚队员在其他队员触球前再次触球（用手除外）：

- 由对方在犯规发生地点踢间接任意球（参见规则第十三章—任意球的位置）。

主罚队员在其他队员触球前故意手球：

- 由对方在犯规发生地点踢直接任意球（参见规则第十三章—任意球的位置），并记录该队1次累计犯规。

当球向前移动后被场外因素触及：

- 应重踢。

球从守门员、横梁或球门柱弹回比赛场地内，接着被场外因素触及：

- 裁判员停止比赛。
- 在被场外因素触及的地点坠球重新开始比赛。如果球在罚球区内触及场外因素情况除外，遇到这种情况，其中一名裁判员应在比赛停止时距球所处地点最近的罚球区线上坠球重新开始比赛。

比赛中，当球在未触及球门柱、横梁或队员前破裂或破损：

- 应重踢。

A kick-in is a method of restarting play.

A kick-in is awarded to the opponents of the player who last touches the ball when the whole of the ball crosses the touch line, either on the ground or in the air, or touches the ceiling of the hall.

A goal may not be scored directly from a kick-in.

Position of the players

The opponents must be:

- on the pitch
- at a distance of no less than 5m from the place on the touch line where the kick-in is taken

Procedure

There is one type of procedure:

- kick-in

Position of kick-in

At the moment of delivering the ball, the kicker:

- has one foot on the touch line or on the ground outside the pitch
- kicks the ball, which must be stationary, either from the point where it left the pitch or on the ground outside it at a distance no greater than 25cm from that point
- delivers the ball within four seconds of being ready to do so

The ball in play is when it enters the pitch.

踢界外球是重新开始比赛的一种方法。

当球的整体无论从地面或空中越过边线或击中天花板时，判由最后触球队员的对方队踢界外球。

踢界外球直接进球得分无效。

队员的位置

对方队员必须：

- 在场上。
- 距界外球踢球地点所处边线至少5米。

程序

只有一种类型的程序：

- 踢界外球。

踢界外球的位置

在踢出界外球的一瞬间，踢球队员：

- 一只脚站在边线或边线外的地上。
- 将球放定在球出界的地点上，或从这一点向外不超过25厘米处踢界外球。
- 在准备好后须在4秒钟内将球踢出。

当球进入场地比赛即为进行。

Infringements and sanctions

If, when a kick-in is taken, an opponent is closer to the ball than the required distance:

- the kick-in is retaken by the same team and the offending player is cautioned, unless the advantage can be applied or an offence punishable by a free kick or penalty kick is committed by the opposing team of the player taking the kick-in

If an opponent unfairly distracts or impedes the player taking the kick-in:

- he is cautioned for unsporting behaviour

For any other infringement of the procedure for the kick-in:

- the kick-in is taken by a player of the opposing team

Kick-in taken by a player other than the goalkeeper

If the ball is in play and the player taking the kick-in touches the ball again (except with his hands) before it has touched another player:

- an indirect free kick is awarded to the opposing team, to be taken from the place where the infringement occurred (see Law 13 – Position of free kick)

If the ball is in play and the player taking the kick-in deliberately handles the ball before it has touched another player:

- a direct free kick is awarded to the opposing team, to be taken from the place where the infringement occurred (see Law 13 – Position of free kick) and his team is sanctioned with an accumulated foul

违规与判罚

如果当踢界外球时，对方队员距踢球地点小于规定的距离时：

- 由同一队重新踢界外球，并警告违规队员，除非此时适用有利条款或踢界外球的对方球队犯有可被判罚直接任意球或球点球的犯规。

如果对方队员不正当地阻挡踢球或分散踢界外球队员注意力：

- 他将因非体育行为被警告。

对于其他任何违反踢界外球程序的行为：

- 由对方踢界外球。

除守门员之外队员踢界外球

如果比赛进行后，踢界外球队员在其他队员触球前再次触球（用手除外）：

- 由对方球队在犯规发生地点踢间接任意球（参见规则第十三章—任意球的位置）。

如果比赛进行后，踢界外球队员在其他队员触球前故意用手触球：

- 由对方球队在犯规发生地点踢直接任意球（参见规则第十三章—任意球的位置），并记录该队1次累计犯规。

- a penalty kick is awarded if the infringement is committed inside the penalty area of the player taking the kick-in and his team is sanctioned with an accumulated foul

Kick-in taken by the goalkeeper

If the ball is in play and the goalkeeper touches the ball again (except with his hands) before it has touched another player:

- an indirect free kick is awarded to the opposing team, to be taken from the place where the infringement occurred (see Law 13 – Position of free kick)

If the ball is in play and the goalkeeper deliberately handles the ball before it has touched another player:

- a direct free kick is awarded to the opposing team if the infringement occurred outside the goalkeeper's penalty area, to be taken from the place where the infringement occurred (see Law 13 – Position of free kick) and his team is sanctioned with an accumulated foul
- an indirect free kick is awarded to the opposing team if the infringement occurred inside the goalkeeper's penalty area, to be taken from the penalty area line at the point nearest to where the infringement occurred (see Law 13 – Position of free kick)

- 如果犯规发生地点在踢界外球队员本方罚球区内，则判罚球点球，并记录该队1次累计犯规。

守门员踢界外球

如果比赛进行后，守门员在其他队员触球前再次触球（用手除外）：

- 由对方球队在犯规发生地点踢间接任意球（参见规则第十三章—任意球的位置）。

如果在比赛进行后，守门员在其他队员触球之前故意用手触球：

- 如果犯规发生地点在守门员本方罚球区外，由对方在犯规发生地点踢直接任意球（参见规则第十三章—任意球的位置），并记录该队1次累计犯规。
- 如果犯规发生地点在守门员本方罚球区内，由对方在距离犯规发生地点最近的罚球区线上踢间接任意球（参见规则第十三章—任意球的位置）。

The goal clearance is a method of restarting play.

A goal clearance is awarded when the whole of the ball passes over the goal line, either on the ground or in the air, having last touched a player of the attacking team, and a goal is not scored in accordance with Law 10.

A goal may not be scored directly from a goal clearance.

Position of the players

The opponents must be:

- on the pitch and outside the penalty area of the team taking the goal clearance until the ball is in play

Procedure

- The ball is thrown from any point inside the penalty area by the goalkeeper of the defending team
- The goalkeeper of the defending team takes the goal clearance within four seconds of being ready to do so
- The ball is in play when it is thrown directly out of the penalty area by the goalkeeper of the defending team

Infringements and sanctions

If the ball is not thrown directly out of the penalty area from a goal clearance:

- the clearance is retaken, but the four-second count is not reset and continues once the goalkeeper is ready to retake it

掷球门球是重新开始比赛的一种方法。

当球的整体无论从地面或空中越过球门线，而最后触球者为攻方队员，且根据规则第十章不是进球得分时，应判为掷球门球。

掷球门球直接进球得分无效。

队员位置

对方队员必须：

- 在比赛场地内，在掷球门球队罚球区外直到比赛进行。

程序

- 由守方守门员在罚球区内任何一点用手掷球。
- 在准备好后，守方守门员应在4秒内将球掷出。
- 当球被守方守门员直接掷出罚球区，比赛即为进行。

违规与判罚

如果球未被直接掷出罚球区进入比赛：

- 重掷。一旦守门员准备好再次掷球门球，4秒计时应继续进行。

If the ball is in play and the goalkeeper touches the ball again (except with his hands) before it has touched another player:

• an indirect free kick is awarded to the opposing team, to be taken from the place where the infringement occurred (see Law 13 - Position of free kick)

If the ball is in play and the goalkeeper deliberately handles the ball before it has touched another player:

• a direct free kick is awarded to the opposing team if the infringement occurred outside the goalkeeper's penalty area, to be taken from the place where the infringement occurred (see Law 13 – Position of free kick) and his team is sanctioned with an accumulated foul

• an indirect free kick is awarded to the opposing team if the infringement occurred inside the goalkeeper's penalty area, to be taken from the penalty area line at the point nearest to where infringement occurred (see Law 13 – Position of free kick)

If the ball is in play and the goalkeeper touches it again in his own half of the pitch after it has been deliberately played to him by a team-mate without an opponent playing or touching it:

• an indirect free kick is awarded to the opposing team, to be taken from the place where the infringement occurred (see Law 13 - Position of free kick)

If the goal clearance is not taken within four seconds:

• an indirect free kick is awarded to the opposing team, to be taken from the penalty area line at the place nearest to where the infringement occurred (see Law 13 – Position of free kick)

如果比赛进行后，守门员在其他队员触球前再次触球（用手除外）：

- 由对方在犯规发生地点踢间接任意球（参见规则第十三章—任意球的位置）。

如果比赛进行后，守门员在其他队员触球前故意用手触球：

- 如果犯规发生地点在守门员本方罚球区外，由对方在犯规发生地点踢直接任意球（参见规则第十三章—任意球的位置），并记录该队1次累计犯规。
- 如果犯规发生地点在守门员本方罚球区内，由对方在距犯规发生地点最近的罚球区线上踢间接任意球（参见规则第十三章—任意球的位置）。

如果比赛进行后，在对方队员传或触球前，守门员在本方半场再次触及同队队员故意传给他的球：

- 由对方在犯规发生地点踢间接任意球（参见规则第十三章—任意球的位置）。

如果没有在4秒内掷出球门球：

- 由对方在距离犯规发生地点最近的罚球区线上踢间接任意球（参见规则第十三章—任意球的位置）。

If the goal clearance is taken with attacking players inside the penalty area:

- the clearance is retaken if any of the attacking players touches the ball or prevents the clearance from being taken properly

In the event of any other infringements of this Law:

- the goal clearance is retaken. If the infringement has been committed by the team taking the clearance, the four-second count is not reset and continues once the goalkeeper is ready to retake the clearance

如果在掷球门球时，对方队员处于罚球区内：

- 如果对方其中一名队员触球或者阻碍守门员掷球门球，应重掷球门球。

对于其他任何违反此规则的：

- 判重掷球门球。如果掷球门球队一方违规，在守门员准备好再次掷球门球时，4秒计时继续进行。

The corner kick is a method of restarting play.

A corner kick is awarded when the whole of the ball passes over the goal line, either on the ground or in the air, having last touched a player of the defending team, and a goal is not scored in accordance with Law 10.

A goal may be scored directly from a corner kick, but only against the opposing team.

Position of the ball and the players

The ball must be:

- inside the corner arc nearest to the point where the ball crossed the goal line

The opponents must be:

- on the pitch at least 5m from the corner arc until the ball is in play

Procedure

- The ball must be kicked by a player of the attacking team
- The team taking the kick must deliver the ball within four seconds of being ready to do so
- The ball is in play when it is kicked and moves

角球是重新开始比赛的一种方法。

当球的整体无论从地面或空中越过球门线，而最后触球者为守方队员，且根据规则第十章不是进球得分时，应判为角球。

角球直接进入对方球门得分有效。

球和队员的位置

球必须：

- 在距球越过球门线最近一侧的角球弧内。

对方队员必须：

- 在比赛场地内距角球弧至少5米直到比赛进行。

程序

- 必须由攻方队员踢球。
- 踢角球一方必须在准备好后4秒内将球踢出。
- 当球被踢并移动时即为比赛进行。

Infringements and sanctions

If, when a corner kick is taken, an opponent is closer to the ball than the required distance:

- the corner kick is retaken by the same team and the offending player is cautioned, unless the advantage can be applied or an offence punishable by a free kick or penalty kick is committed by the defending team

If an opponent unfairly distracts or impedes the player taking the corner kick:

- he is cautioned for unsporting behaviour

If the corner kick is not taken within four seconds:

- a goal clearance is awarded to the opposing team

In the event of any other infringement of the procedure or the position of the ball:

- the kick is retaken. If the infringement has been committed by the team taking the kick, the four-second count is not reset and continues once the kicker is ready to retake the kick

Corner kick taken by a player other than the goalkeeper

If the ball is in play and the player taking the kick touches the ball again (except with his hands) before it has touched another player:

- an indirect free kick is awarded to the opposing team, to be taken from the place where the infringement occurred (see Law 13 – Position of free kick)

违规与判罚

如果在踢角球时，对方队员没有退出规定的距离：

- 由同一队重新踢角球，并警告犯规队员，除非此时适用有利条款或守方队员犯有可被判罚直接任意球或球点球的犯规。

如果在踢角球时对方不正当地阻挡或分散主罚队员的注意力：

- 他将因非体育行为被警告。

如果角球没有在4秒内踢出：

- 判由对方掷球门球。

对于其他任何违反程序或其位置行为：

- 判重踢角球。如果踢角球方违规，在主罚队员准备好重新踢角球时，4秒计时继续进行。

除守门员外的场上队员踢角球

如果比赛进行后，踢球队员在其他队员触球前再次触球（用手除外）：

- 由对方在犯规发生地点踢间接任意球（参见规则第十三章—任意球的位置）。

If the ball is in play and the kicker deliberately handles the ball before it has touched another player:

- a direct free kick is awarded to the opposing team, to be taken from the place where the infringement occurred (see Law 13 – Position of free kick), and his team is sanctioned with an accumulated foul
- a penalty kick is awarded if the infringement was committed inside the penalty area of the player taking the kick and his team is sanctioned with an accumulated foul

Corner kick taken by the goalkeeper

If the ball is in play and the goalkeeper touches the ball again (except with his hands), before it has touched another player:

- an indirect free kick is awarded to the opposing team, to be taken from the place where the infringement occurred (see Law 13 – Position of free kick)

If the ball is in play and the goalkeeper deliberately handles the ball before it has touched another player:

- a direct free kick is awarded to the opposing team if the infringement occurred outside the goalkeeper's penalty area, to be taken from the place where the infringement occurred (see Law 13 – Position of free kick), and his team is sanctioned with an accumulated foul
- an indirect free kick is awarded to the opposing team if the infringement occurred inside the goalkeeper's penalty area, to be taken from the place where the infringement occurred (see Law 13 – Position of free kick)

如果比赛进行后，踢球队员在其他队员触球前故意用手触球：

- 由对方在犯规发生地点踢直接任意球（参见规则第十三章—任意球的位置），并记录该队1次累计犯规；
- 如果犯规发生地点在踢球队员本方罚球区内，则判罚球点球，并记录该队1次累计犯规。

守门员踢角球

如果比赛进行后，守门员在其他队员触球前再次触球（用手除外）：

- 由对方在犯规发生地点踢间接任意球（参见规则第十三章—任意球的位置）。

如果比赛进行后，守门员在其他队员触球前故意用手触球：

- 如果犯规发生地点在守门员本方罚球区外，由对方在犯规发生地点踢直接任意球（参见规则第十三章—任意球的位置），并记录该队1次累计犯规。
- 如果犯规发生地点在守门员本方罚球区内，由对方在距犯规发生地点最近的罚球区线上踢间接任意球（参见规则第十三章－任意球的位置）。

Away goals, extra time and kicks from the penalty mark are the three methods approved for determining the winning team where competition rules require there to be a winning team after a match has been drawn. Extra time and kicks from the penalty mark are not part of the match.

Away goals

Competition rules may provide that where teams play each other home and away, if the aggregate score is equal after the second match, any goals scored on the pitch of the opposing team will count double.

Extra time

Competition rules may provide for two further equal periods, of three or five minutes each, to be played. The conditions of Law 8 will apply. The competition regulations must state the precise duration of the two equal periods of extra time.

Kicks from the penalty mark

Competition rules may provide for kicks from the penalty mark in accordance with the procedure stipulated below.

客场进球规则、加时赛和踢球点球决胜是根据竞赛规程的要求，当一场比赛或主客场比赛打平后需要决出胜队时采用的三种被批准的决胜方法。加时赛和踢球点球决胜不是比赛的一部分。

客场进球规则

竞赛规程若规定比赛采用主客场制，如果第二场比赛后两队总比分相同，则任何在客场进球数将加倍计算。

加时赛

竞赛规程可以规定再进行两个半场时间相等的比赛，每半场时间为3或5分钟。适用规则第八章的有关规定。竞赛规程应规定加时赛的确切时间。

踢球点球决胜

竞赛规程可以规定按照以下踢球点球程序决定比赛胜负。

Procedure

- The referee chooses the goal at which the kicks will be taken
- The referee tosses a coin and the team whose captain wins the toss decides whether to take the first or the second kick
- The referee, the second referee, the third referee and the timekeeper keep a record of the kicks being taken
- Subject to the conditions explained below, both teams take three kicks
- The kicks are taken alternately by the teams
- If, before both teams have taken three kicks, one has scored more goals than the other could score even if it were to complete its three kicks, no more kicks are taken
- If, after both teams have taken three kicks, both have scored the same number of goals, or have not scored any goals, kicks continue to be taken in the same order until one team has scored a goal more than the other from the same number of kicks
- All players and substitutes are authorised to take the penalty kicks
- A goalkeeper may be replaced by any player while kicks are being taken from the penalty mark
- Each kick is taken by a different player and all eligible players must take a kick before any player can take a second kick

程序

- 裁判员选定用于踢球点球的球门。
- 裁判员组织掷币，掷币获胜的球队队长决定本队是否先踢球点球。
- 裁判员、第二裁判员、第三裁判员和计时员负责记录罚球点球执行情况。
- 按照下列解释，两队应各踢3次。
- 双方轮流踢球点球。
- 如果两队在踢满3次前，一队的进球数已多于另一队踢满3次时可能的进球数，则不需再踢。
- 如果两队均已踢满3次，双方进球数相同或均未进球，则按相同顺序轮流踢球点球，直至双方踢球次数相同，而一队较另一队多进一球时为止。
- 所有队员和替补队员均有资格踢球点球。
- 在踢球点球过程中，守门员可由任何队员替换。
- 每次应由不同的队员踢球点球，直至双方符合资格的队员均踢过一次后，方可踢第二次。

- An eligible player may change places with the goalkeeper at any time when kicks from the penalty mark are being taken, provided that the referee is informed and his equipment is suitable
- Only the eligible players, including the goalkeepers, the referees and the third referee are permitted to remain on the pitch when kicks from the penalty mark are being taken
- All eligible players, except the player taking the kick and the two goalkeepers, must remain in the opposite half of the pitch with the third referee
- The goalkeeper who is the team-mate of the kicker must remain on the opposite side to the substitution zones, on the pitch level with the penalty mark and at least 5m from it
- Unless otherwise stated, the Futsal Laws of the Game and guidelines of the FIFA Refereeing Department apply when kicks from the penalty mark are being taken
- If, at the end of the match or extra time and before the kicks start to be taken from the penalty mark, one team has a greater number of players, including substitutes, than its opponents, it must reduce its numbers to equate with that of its opponents and the team captain must inform the referee of the name and number of each player excluded

- 在踢球点球过程中，符合资格的队员可与守门员互换位置，只要事先通知裁判员且其装备符合规定。
- 在踢球点球过程中，只允许符合资格的队员，包括守门员和裁判员、第三裁判员留在比赛场地内。
- 除踢球点球队员和两名守门员外，其他所有符合资格的队员必须和第三裁判员一起位于比赛场地另一半场内。
- 踢球点球队员一方的守门员须位于替换区对面，与罚球点齐平并距球至少5米的比赛场地内。
- 除非另有所述，室内五人制足球竞赛规则诠释及裁判员指南同样适用踢球点球决胜的过程。
- 如果在比赛或加时赛结束时并在踢球点球决胜之前，某队的队员（包括替补队员）人数多于另一队，该队必须减去多出的人数与对方人数一致，该队的队长应通知裁判员被排除队员的名字和号码。

- If a team must reduce its numbers to equate with that of its opponents, it may exclude the goalkeepers as players eligible to take the penalty kicks
- A goalkeeper excluded from taking penalty kicks in order to equate the number of players of his team with that of its opponents, i.e. who is located in his technical area, may replace his team's goalkeeper at any time
- Before the start of the kicks from the penalty mark, the referee must ensure that an equal number of players from each team eligible to take the penalty kicks remains in the other half of the pitch

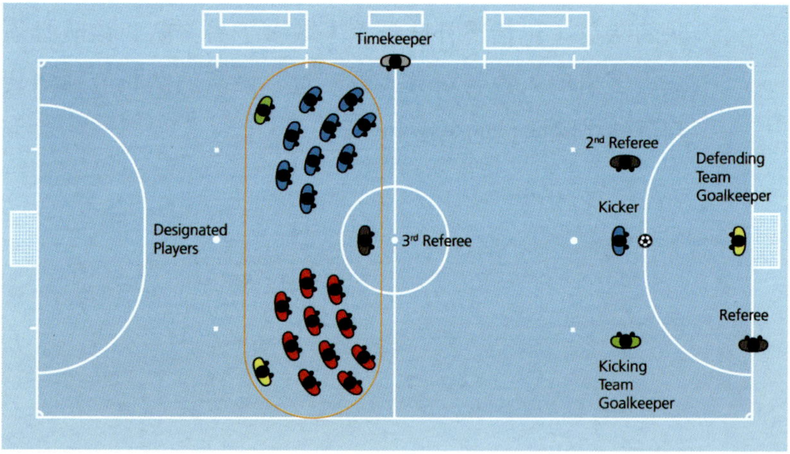

- 如果一球队必须减少队员人数以期达到和对方球队人数相同，则守门员可以像符合规定的队员一样被排除在踢球点球之外。
- 如果一守门员被球队排除在踢球点球之外，以期达到本队与对方球队人数相同，他可以留在技术区域内，随时替换本队守门员。
- 在开始踢球点球决胜之前，裁判员必须确保两队符合踢球点球资格的队员人数相等，且位于另一半场内。

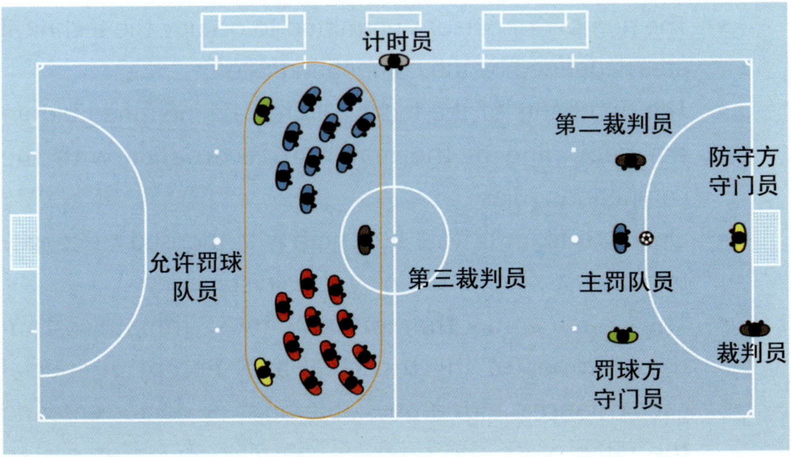

The technical area is a special zone for technical staff and substitutes.

While the size and position of technical areas may differ between facilities, the following notes are issued for general guidance:

- The technical area extends 1m on either side of the designated seated area and extends forward up to a distance of 75cm from the touch line
- It is recommended that markings are used to define this area
- The number of persons permitted to occupy the technical area is defined by the competition rules
- The occupants of the technical area are identified before the beginning of the match in accordance with the competition rules
- Only one team official at a time is authorised to convey tactical instructions and may remain standing
- The coach and other officials must remain within the confines of the technical area except in special circumstances, e.g. a physiotherapist or doctor entering the pitch, with the referees' permission, to assess an injured player or organise his removal from the pitch
- The coach and other occupants of the technical area must behave in a responsible manner, avoiding any obstruction of the players' and referees' movements

技术区域是技术官员和替补队员所在的特殊区域。

技术区域的大小和位置可以根据场地设施情况而不同，以下是一般性指导：

- 技术区域的范围是指，从替补席两侧向外1米及向前延伸至距边线75厘米的区域。
- 建议用标记线明确该区域。
- 技术区域内的人数由竞赛规程决定。
- 根据竞赛规程，在比赛前确认替补席内的具体人员。
- 每次只允许一名球队官员在技术区域内站着进行技术性指导。
- 教练员和其他官员必须在替补席指定位置，除非发生特殊情况，如场上队员受伤，裁判员允许理疗师或医生进场察看伤情时。
- 教练员或其他在技术区域内的人员要对自己的行为负责，避免任何阻碍队员和裁判员移动的行为。

- The substitutes and the fitness coach may warm up during a match in the zone provided for this purpose, as long as they do not obstruct the movements of players and referees and they behave responsibly

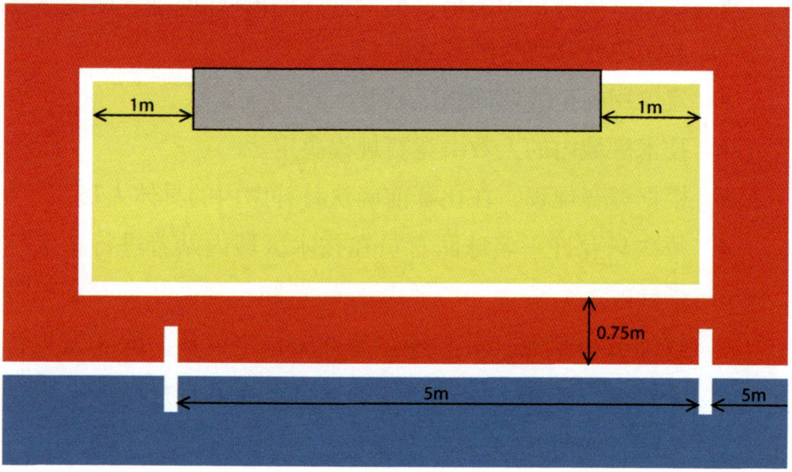

- 比赛期间替补队员和体能教练员可以在预设区域内热身，只要他们对自己行为负责，并且不阻碍队员和裁判员的移动。

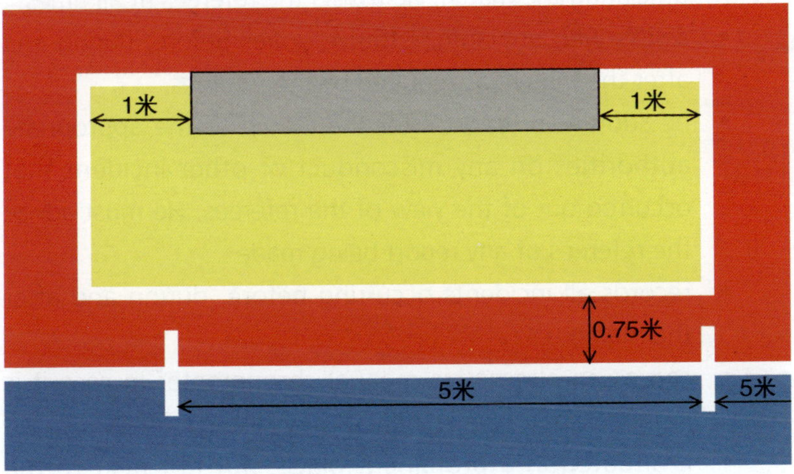

The reserve assistant referee:

- is appointed under the competition rules and replaces the timekeeper if any of the referees is unable to continue officiating the match. He assists the referees at all times
- assists with any administrative duties before, during and after the match, as required by the referees
- he submits a report after the match to the appropriate authorities on any misconduct or other incident that occurred out of the view of the referees. He must advise the referees of any report being made
- records all incidents occurring before, during and after the match
- carries an alternative manual chronometer in case it is required due to an incident of any kind
- is situated in a prominent place, but not next to the assistant referees

候补助理裁判员：

- 根据竞赛规程任命。如果任何裁判员不能继续执法比赛时替代计时员。他在任何时候都应协助裁判员。
- 根据裁判员的要求，在赛前、赛中或赛后协助承担管理性的职责。
- 他在比赛后必须向相关主办机构就任何不正当行为或裁判员视线外发生的事件提交报告。他必须向裁判员提交的任何报告提供建议。
- 记录赛前、赛中和赛后发生的所有意外事件。
- 携带一个备用手工计时器，以防由于任何事故发生而作为备用。
- 位于显著的位置，但非助理裁判员旁边。

The referees must give the signals listed below, bearing in mind that there are signals that only one of the referees must make and one signal that both referees must make at the same time.

The assistant referees must give the signals for a time-out and the fifth accumulated foul.

Signals by only one of the referees

Kick-off/restart of play

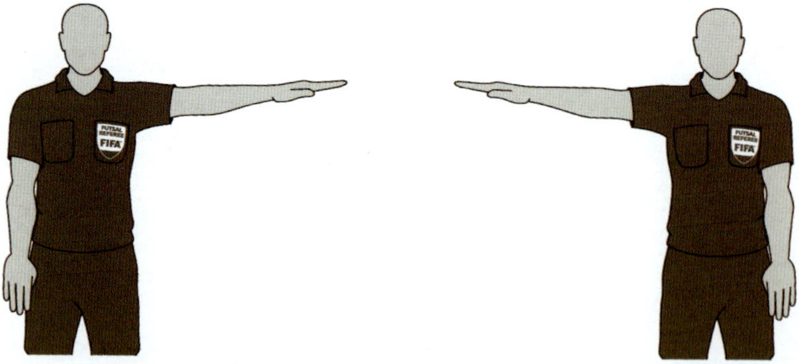

Direct free kick/penalty kick

裁判员必须做出以下手势，但需注意一些手势仅是一名裁判员必须示意的、一些手势是两名裁判员必须同时示意的。

助理裁判员必须用手势示意暂停或第5次累计犯规。

仅由一名裁判员使用的手势

开球/比赛重新开始

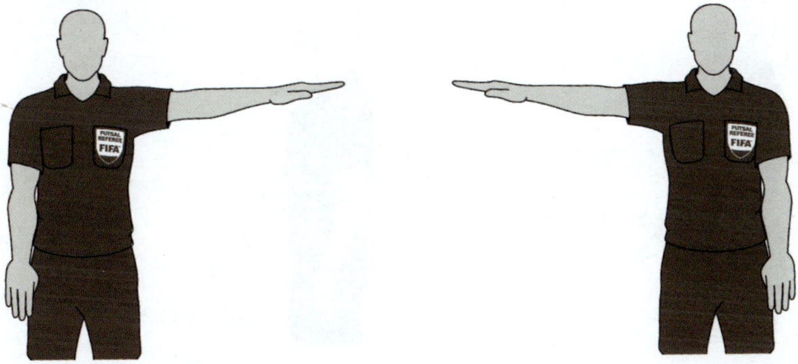

直接任意球/罚球点球

Kick-in (1)

Kick-in (2)

Corner kick (1)

Corner kick (2)

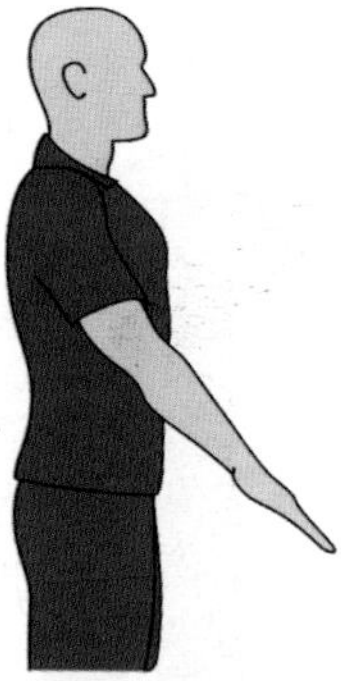

Goal clearance (1)

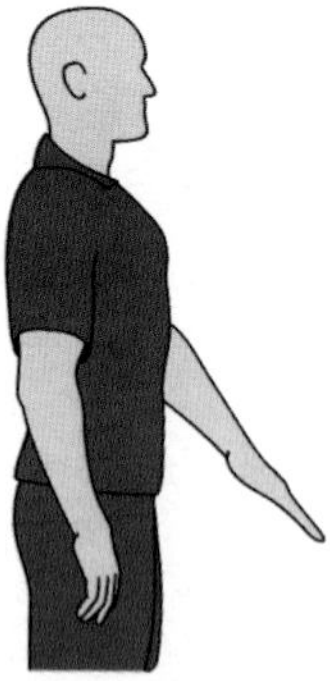

Goal clearance (2)

踢界外球（1）

踢界外球（2）

角球（1）

角球（2）

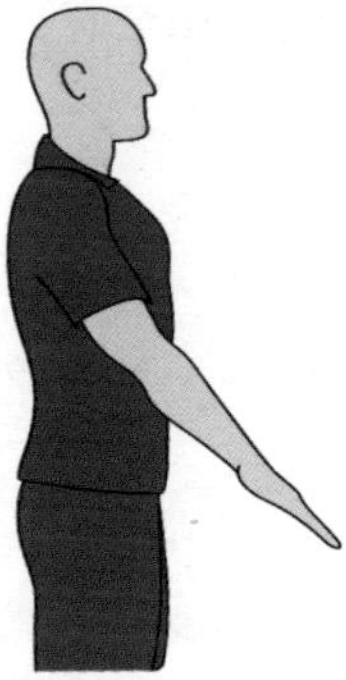

掷球门球（1）

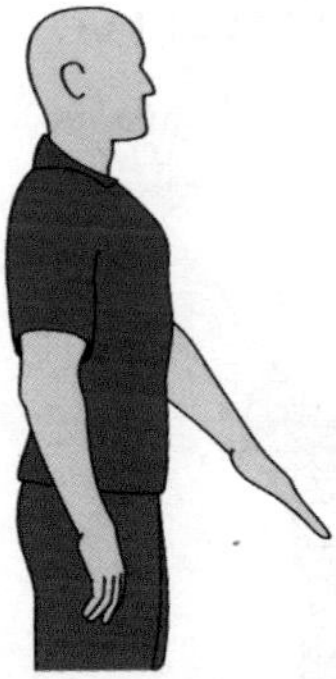

掷球门球（2）

Time-out

Four-second count (1)

Four-second count (2)

Fifth accumulated foul

暂停

4秒钟计时（1）

4秒钟计时（2）

第5次累计犯规

Advantage after accumulated foul

Advantage after non-accumulated foul

累计犯规的有利

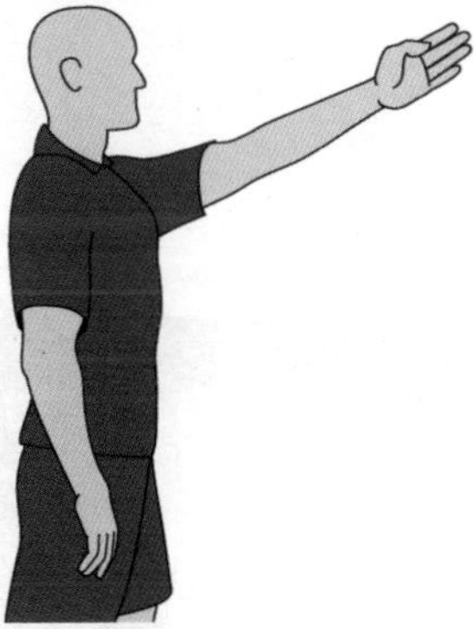

非累计犯规的有利

Accumulated foul after
the advantage has been applied (1)

Accumulated foul after
the advantage has been applied (2)

Accumulated foul after
the advantage has been applied (3)

Accumulated foul after
the advantage has been applied (4)

有利条款运用后的累计犯规（1）

有利条款运用后的累计犯规（2）

有利条款运用后的累计犯规（3）

有利条款运用后的累计犯规（4）

Caution (yellow card)

Sending-off (red card)

Indirect free kick

警告（黄牌）

罚令出场（红牌）

间接任意球

Number of player – 1

Number of player – 2

Number of player – 3

Number of player – 4

Number of player –5

Number of player –6

队员号码–1

队员号码–2

队员号码–3

队员号码–4

队员号码–5

队员号码–6

Number of player – 7

Number of player –8

Number of player –9

Number of player – 10

Number of player –11

Number of player –12

队员号码–7

队员号码–8

队员号码–9

队员号码–10

队员号码–11

队员号码–12

Number of player –13

Number of player –14

Number of player –15

Goal

Own goal (1)

Own goal (2)

队员号码–13

队员号码–14

队员号码–15

进球

乌龙球（1）

乌龙球（2）

Signal by both referees on restarting play

Indirect free kick

Signals by the assistant referees

Time-out

Fifth accumulated foul

比赛重新开始时两名裁判员同时使用的手势

间接任意球

助理裁判员的信号

暂停

第5次累计犯规

Interpretation of the Futsal Laws of the Game and Guidelines for Referees

室内五人制足球竞赛规则诠释及裁判员指南

Pitch surface

Matches must be played on flat surfaces, according to the rules of the competition.

Artificial turf

The use of artificial turf is not permitted in competition matches between representative teams of member associations affiliated to FIFA or international club competition matches.

Pitch markings

It is not permissible to mark the pitch with broken lines.

If a player makes unauthorised marks on the pitch, he must be cautioned for unsporting behaviour. If the referees notice this being done during the match, they must stop play if they cannot apply the advantage, caution the offending player for unsporting behaviour and order play to be restarted with an indirect free kick to the opposing team from the position of the ball when play was stopped (see Law 13 – Position of free kick).

An attempt should be made to use only the lines stipulated in Law 1 to mark the pitch, but since futsal is usually played in halls equipped for various sports, lines other than those used for football must be accepted, provided that they do not confuse the players and referee

场地表面

根据竞赛规程，比赛应在表面平坦的球场进行。

人造草坪

人造草坪不能在FIFA会员协会代表队之间，以及国际性俱乐部比赛中使用。

场地标记

在画场地时不允许有断裂的标记线。

如果发现某队员未经允许在场内做标记，则该队员因非体育行为必须被警告。如果在赛中裁判员注意到了类似行为，若有利条款不适用，裁判员应停止比赛并因非体育行为警告该队员，然后在比赛停止时球所在地点踢间接任意球重新开始比赛（参见规则第十三章—任意球的位置）。

场地画线应根据竞赛规则第一章的有关要求进行标记。由于举办室内五人制足球比赛的场地大多数情况下都同时用于多种运动项目，如果这些画线未干扰队员和裁判员，则可以被接受。

No lines or markings are allowed within 5m of the second penalty mark and inside the penalty area to indicate the distance that the defending goalkeeper must retreat while a kick from the second penalty mark is being taken.

Goals

If the crossbar becomes displaced or broken, play is stopped until it has been repaired or replaced in position. If it is not possible to repair the crossbar, the match must be abandoned. The use of a rope to replace the crossbar is not permitted. If the crossbar can be repaired, the match is restarted with a dropped ball from the position of the ball when play was stopped, unless play was stopped inside the penalty area, in which case one of the referees drops the ball on the penalty area line at the point nearest to where the ball was located when play was stopped.

Safety

The competition rules state the distance that must exist between the boundary lines of the pitch (touch lines and goal lines) and the barriers separating the spectators, but always in such a way as to protect the participants' safety.

Advertising on the pitch

If the competition rules do not prohibit it, advertising on the floor of the pitch is permitted, provided that it does not confuse the players or referees and it enables the boundary lines stipulated in the Futsal Laws of the Game to be seen.

从第二罚球点罚球时，距第二罚球点5米范围内和罚球区内不允许用画线或标记示意守方守门员必须退出的距离。

球门

如果球门横梁移位或破损，应停止比赛直到横梁修复或移回原位。如果横梁无法修复，比赛应取消。不允许用绳子代替横梁。如果横梁能被修复，应在比赛停止时球所在地点坠球重新开始比赛，除非比赛停止时球在罚球区内，在此情况下则由其中一名裁判员在比赛停止时距球所处地点最近的罚球区线上坠球重新开始比赛。

安全

竞赛规程应明确比赛场地边界线（边线、球门线）和用于隔离观众的障碍物之间的必需距离，但以上措施须以保护比赛参与者的安全为前提。

场地广告

如果竞赛规程未禁止，可允许场地地面广告，只要其不对裁判员及球员造成干扰，并且确保可见室内五人制足球竞赛规则所要求的边界线。

Advertising on the goal nets

If the competition rules do not prohibit it, advertising on the goal nets is permitted, provided that it does not confuse the players or referees.

Advertising in the technical areas

If the competition rules do not prohibit it, advertising on the floor of the technical areas is permitted, provided that it does not confuse the occupants of said areas, the third referee or the referees.

Comercial advertising around the pitch

Upright advertising shall be at least:

1. 1m (1yd) from the touch lines, except in the technical area and substitution zone, in which all advertising is prohibited.

2. the same distance from the goal line as the depth of the goal net.

3. 1m (1yd) from the goal net.

球门网广告

如果竞赛规程未禁止，可允许球门网上的广告，只要其不对裁判员及球员造成干扰。

技术区域广告

如果竞赛规程未禁止，可允许技术区域内的地面广告，只要其不对该区域内人员、第三裁判员或裁判员造成干扰。

比赛场地周围的商业广告

竖立式广告应符合以下条件：

1. 距边线1米（1码），但是在技术区域和替换区禁止有广告。

2. 距球门线的距离与球网的深度相同。

3. 距球门网1米（1码）。

Additional balls

Additional balls may be placed around the pitch for use during a match provided that they meet the requirements of Law 2 and their use is under the control of the referees.

Extra balls on the pitch

If an extra ball enters the pitch while the ball is in play, the referees must stop the match only if the extra ball interferes with play. Play must be restarted with a dropped ball from the position of the ball when play was stopped, unless play was stopped inside the penalty area, in which case one of the referees drops the ball on the penalty area line at the point nearest to where the ball was located when play was stopped.

If an extra ball enters the pitch while the ball is in play without interfering with play, the referees must have it removed at the earliest possible opportunity.

Burst or defective ball

If the ball bursts or becomes defective after striking one of the goalposts or the

crossbar and enters the goal, the referees award the goal.

备用球

比赛中可将多个备用球摆放在场地四周，只要这些球符合规则第二章的有关规定，且在裁判员的控制下使用。

场上多余的球

如果比赛进行中有球进入比赛场地，只要这个球干扰了比赛，裁判员就必须停止比赛。比赛应在停止时球所在地点以坠球方式重新开始，除非比赛停止时球在罚球区内，在此情况下则由其中一名裁判员在比赛停止时距球所处地点最近的罚球区线上坠球重新开始比赛。

如果比赛进行中有球进入比赛场地，但并没有干扰比赛，裁判员应在可能的情况下尽早将其清出场外。

球的破裂或破损

如果球在触碰球门横梁或其中一个门柱破裂或破损后进入球门，裁判员应判得分有效。

Substitution procedure

- A substitution may be made during play or during a stoppage in play, except during a time-out
- The player being substituted does not need to obtain the referees' permission to leave the pitch
- The referees do not need to authorise the substitute to enter the pitch
- Before entering the pitch, the substitute waits for the player he is replacing to leave the pitch
- The player being substituted is required to leave the pitch via his own team's substitution zone, except if he is already outside the pitch with the referees' permission or for the reasons provided in Laws 3 or 4
- Permission to proceed with a substitution may be refused under certain circumstances, e.g. if the substitute does not have his equipment in order
- A substitute who has not completed the substitution procedure by setting foot on the pitch via his substitution zone cannot restart play by taking a kick-in, corner kick, etc. until he completes the substitution procedure
- If a player who is about to be replaced refuses to leave the pitch, the substitution cannot be made
- If a substitution is made during the half-time interval or before any of the periods of extra time, the substitute may enter the pitch via the substitution zone after informing the third referee or the referee, if there is no third referee

替补程序

- 替换队员可在比赛进行中或停止时进行，但比赛暂停时不允许替换。
- 被替换队员不需要获得裁判员的许可即可离开场地。
- 无需裁判员许可，替补队员即可进入场地。
- 替补队员必须在被替换队员完全离场后方可进入场地。
- 被替换队员必须由本方半场替换离场，除非在裁判员许可下，或者由于规则第三章、第四章规定的原因，该队员已经离场。
- 在特殊情况下可拒绝某球队的替换要求，例如，替补队员的装备不符合规定。
- 当替补队员未通过本队替换区进入场地完成替补程序时，不能以踢界外球、角球等重新开始比赛，除非其按规定完成替补程序。
- 一名被要求替换下场的队员拒绝下场，替换不能完成。
- 如果半场休息时或在任何加时赛半场前进行替换，该替换队员应在通知第三裁判员或裁判员后经替换区进入比赛场地。

Extra persons on the pitch

Outside agents

Anyone not indicated on the list of players before the start of the match as a player or substitute or who is not a team official is deemed to be an outside agent.

If an outside agent enters the pitch:

- the referees must stop play (although not immediately if the outside agent does not interfere with play)
- the referees must have him removed from the pitch and its immediate surroundings
- if the referees stop the match, they must restart play with a dropped ball from the position of the ball when play was stopped, unless play was stopped inside the penalty area, in which case one of the referees drops the ball on the penalty area line at the point nearest to where the ball was located when play was stopped

Team officials

If a team official enters the pitch:

- the referees must stop play (although not immediately if the team official does not interfere with play or if the advantage can be applied)
- the referees must have him removed from the pitch and if his behaviour is irresponsible, the referees must expel him from the pitch and its immediate surroundings

场上额外人员

场外因素

赛前既未作为队员或替补队员列入比赛名单，又不是球队官员的人都将被认为是场外因素。

如果场外因素进入比赛场地：

- 裁判员停止比赛（如果场外因素未干扰比赛时可不立即执行）。
- 裁判员必须使场外因素离开场地及其附近区域。
- 如果裁判员停止比赛，则应在比赛停止时球所在地点以坠球方式重新开始比赛。除非比赛在罚球区内被停止，在此情况下则由其中一名裁判员在比赛停止时距球所处地点最近的罚球区线上坠球重新开始比赛。

球队官员

如果一球队官员进入比赛场地：

- 裁判员必须停止比赛（如果球队官员未干扰比赛，或在掌握有利时可不立即执行）。
- 裁判员必须使其离开场地。如果该官员行为是不负责任的，则裁判员必须将其逐出场地及其附近区域。

- if the referees stop the match, they must restart play with a dropped ball from the position of the ball when play was stopped, unless play was stopped inside the penalty area, in which case one of the referees drops the ball on the penalty area line at the point nearest to where the ball was located when play was stopped

Players sent off

If a sent-off player enters the pitch:

- the referees must stop play, although not immediately if the sent-off player does not interfere with play or if the advantage can be applied
- the referees must have him removed from the pitch and its immediate surroundings
- if the referees stop the match, they must restart play with a dropped ball from the position of the ball when the match was stopped, unless play was stopped inside the penalty area, in which case one of the referees drops the ball on the penalty area line at the point nearest to where the ball was located when play was stopped

Player outside the pitch

If, after leaving the pitch to correct unauthorised equipment or kit, to be treated for an injury or bleeding, because he has blood on his kit or for any other reason with the referees' permission, a player re-enters pitch without the referees' permission, the referees must:

- stop play, although not immediately if they can apply the advantage

- 如果裁判员停止比赛，则应在比赛停止时球所在地点以坠球方式重新开始比赛。除非比赛在罚球区内被停止，在此情况下则应由其中一名裁判员在比赛停止时距球所处地点最近的罚球区线上坠球重新开始比赛。

被罚令出场的队员

如果被罚令出场的队员进入比赛场地：

- 裁判员必须停止比赛（如果被罚令出场的队员未干扰比赛，或在掌握有利时可不立即执行）。
- 裁判员必须使其离开场地及其附近区域。
- 如果裁判员停止比赛，则应在比赛停止时球所在地点以坠球方式重新开始比赛。除非比赛停止时球在罚球区内，在此情况下则应由其中一名裁判员在比赛停止时距球所处地点最近的罚球区线上坠球重新开始比赛。

场外队员

如果队员由于整理装备、接受受伤或流血治疗、服装上有血渍或其他原因经裁判员允许离开场地之后，在未得到裁判员允许下重新进入场地，则裁判员必须：

- 停止比赛。掌握有利时可不立即执行。

- caution the player for entering the pitch without permission
- order the player to leave the pitch if necessary (e.g. infringement of Law 4)

If the referees stop play, it must be restarted:

- with an indirect free kick to the opposing team from the position of the ball when play was stopped (see Law 13 – Position of free kick) if there is no other infringement
- in accordance with Law 12 if the player also infringes this Law

If a player who is outside the pitch with the referees' permission and who has not been substituted re-enters the pitch without the permission of the referees or the third referee and furthermore commits another cautionable infringement, the referees send him off for a double caution, e.g. the player enters without the permission of the referees or the third referee and trips an opponent in a reckless manner. If this infringement is committed with excessive force, the player is sent off directly.

- 警告该未经允许进入场地的队员。
- 如果必要则令相关队员离场（例如违反规则第四章）。

如果裁判员停止比赛，则按照如下方式重新开始比赛：

- 由对方在比赛停止时球所在地点以间接任意球方式重新开始比赛（参见规则第十三章—任意球的位置）。
- 如果队员违反规则第十二章，则照章重新开始比赛。

如果一队员经裁判员允许下场后，在未被替换下场的情况下，未经裁判员或第三裁判员允许再次进入场地，并且犯有可被警告的犯规，则裁判员应由于第二次警告将其罚令出场。例如，队员在未经裁判员或第三裁判员允许进入场地，并且以鲁莽的方式绊摔对方队员。如果该犯规使用了过分的力量，则该队员应被直接罚令出场。

If the referees stop play, it must be restarted in accordance with Law 12.

If a player accidentally crosses one of the boundary lines of the pitch, he is not deemed to have committed an infringement. If a player leaves the pitch as part of a playing movement, he is not deemed to have committed an infringement.

Substitutes

If a substitute enters the pitch by infringing the substitution procedure or causes his team to be playing with an extra player, the referees, assisted by the assistant referees, must adhere to the following guidelines:

- Stop play, although not immediately if the advantage can be applied
- Caution him for unsporting behaviour if his team plays with an extra player or for infringing the substitution procedure if the substitution was not made correctly
- Send him off if he denies the opposing team a goal or an obvious goalscoring opportunity. The number of players in his team is reduced irrespective of whether the offence consists of an infringement of the substitution procedure or because his team is playing with an extra player, in which case in addition to the substitute sent off, another of the players must leave the pitch so that his team is then playing with one player less, with a new player being introduced as specified in the section of Law 3 entitled "Players and substitutes sent off"

如果裁判员停止比赛，则必须根据规则第十二章的规定重新开始比赛。

如果一队员意外越过场地的一条边界线，则不应认为该队员违规。当队员出场被认为是比赛的一部分时，不应认为该队员违规。

替补队员

如果一球队替补队员违反替补程序进入场地或造成该队场上多一名队员时，裁判员应在助理裁判员的协助下遵循如下条款：

- 停止比赛，但在掌握有利时可不立即执行。
- 警告该队员，若该队员所在球队场上额外多一人，则处罚原因是犯有非体育行为；若出现不正确的替换，则处罚原因是违反替补程序。
- 如果该队员破坏了对方进球或明显的进球得分机会则必须被罚令出场。他所在球队的人数应减少，无论他是违反替补程序还是该队在场上多一人。在后一种情况下，除了将替补队员罚令出场外，该队另外一名队员应离场以使该队少一人，并可根据规则第三章“队员和替补队员被罚令出场”的规定补充队员。

- The substitute must leave the pitch at the first stoppage in the match if he has not left before, either to complete the substitution procedure, if the infringement was for this reason, or to move to the technical area, if his team was playing with an extra player
- If they apply the advantage, stop play once the substitute' s team is in possession of the ball and restart it with an indirect free kick for the opposing team from the position of the ball when play was stopped (see Law 13 – Position of free kick)
- If they apply the advantage and stop play because the opposing team commits an infringement or because the ball leaves the pitch, they must restart play with an indirect free kick to the opponents of the substitute' s team from the position of the ball when play was stopped (see Law 13 – Position of free kick). If necessary, they also take the disciplinary action corresponding to the infringement committed by the opponents of the substitute's team
- If they apply the advantage and another player of the substitute's team commits an infringement punishable by a direct free kick or penalty kick, they sanction the substitute's team with a direct free kick (see Law 13 – Position of free kick) or penalty kick. If necessary, they also take the disciplinary action corresponding to the infringement committed

- 如果该替补队员尚未离开场地，则其必须在比赛下一次停止时离开场地，如果违反替补程序，则可以离场完成替补程序；如果他所在球队场上额外多一人，则可以回到技术区域。
- 如果裁判员掌握有利，应在替补队员所在球队控球时停止比赛，并由对方以间接任意球在比赛停止时球所在地点重新开始比赛（参见规则第十三章—任意球的位置）。
- 如果裁判员掌握有利后因对方球队犯规或球离开场地而停止比赛，则应由替补队员所在球队的对方以间接任意球在比赛停止时球所在地点重新开始比赛（参见规则第十三章—任意球的位置）。如有必要，裁判员也可根据相应的犯规对替补队员所在球队的对方采取纪律处罚。
- 如果裁判员掌握有利，替补队员所在球队的另外一名队员犯有可被判罚直接任意球或球点球的犯规，则替补队员所在球队应被判直接任意球（参见规则第十三章—任意球的位置）。如有必要，裁判员也可根据相应的犯规采取纪律处罚。

- If they apply the advantage and the substitute does not follow the substitution procedure and commits an infringement punishable by a direct free kick or penalty kick, they sanction the substitute's team with a direct free kick (see Law 13 – Position of free kick) or penalty kick. If necessary, they also take the disciplinary action corresponding to the infringement committed
- If they apply the advantage and the substitute's team plays with an extra player, and this player commits an infringement punishable by a direct free kick or penalty kick, they sanction this player's team with an indirect free kick from the position of the ball when play was stopped (see Law 13 – Position of free kick). If necessary, they also take the disciplinary action corresponding to the infringement committed

If a named substitute enters the field of play instead of a named player at the start of the match and the referee or assistant referees are not informed of this change:

- the referees allow the named substitute to continue the match
- no disciplinary sanction is taken against the named substitute
- the referee reports the incident to the appropriate authorities

If a substitute commits a sending-off offence before entering the pitch, the number of players in his team is not reduced and another substitute or the player he was going to replace may enter the pitch

- 如果裁判员掌握有利，但替补队员没有遵循替补程序并犯有可被判罚直接任意球或球点球的犯规，则替补队员所在队应被判直接任意球（参见规则第十三章—任意球的位置）或球点球。如有必要，裁判员也可根据相应的犯规采取纪律处罚。
- 如果裁判员掌握有利，替补队员所在球队额外多一人，且该队员犯有可被判罚直接任意球或球点球的犯规，则该队员所在球队应在比赛停止时球所在地点被判间接任意球（参见规则第十三章—任意球的位置）。如有必要，裁判员也可根据相应的犯规采取纪律处罚。

如果一名提名的替补队员在比赛开始时代替提名的场上队员进入场地参加比赛，而此前没有通知裁判员或助理裁判员：

- 裁判员允许提名的替补队员继续参加比赛。
- 裁判员不应对提名的替补队员进行纪律制裁。
- 裁判员就这一事件向相关机构报告。

如果一替补队员在进入场地前犯有可被罚令出场的犯规，则该队的队员人数不应减少，而该队另外一名替补队员或之前将要被替换下场的队员可进入场地。

Authorised departure from the pitch

IIn addition to a normal substitution, a player may leave the pitch without the referees' permission in the following situations:

- As part of a playing movement whereby he immediately returns to the pitch, i.e. to play the ball or place himself in an advantageous position by dribbling past an opponent. However, it is not permitted to leave the pitch and pass behind one of the goals before re-entering the pitch with the aim of deceiving the opponents; if he does, the referees stop play if they cannot apply the advantage. If they stop play, they must restart it with an indirect free kick from the position of the ball when play was stopped (see Law 13–Position of free kick). The player is cautioned for leaving the pitch without the referees' permission
- Due to injury. The player needs the permission of the referees or the third referee to re-enter the pitch if he has not been substituted. If he is suffering from a bleeding wound, the bleeding must have stopped before he re-enters the pitch and he must be checked by the referees or the third referee
- To correct or put back on his equipment. The player needs the referees' permission to re-enter the pitch if he has not been substituted, and the referees or the third referee must check his equipment before he returns to the match

合法离开比赛场地

除正常的队员替换之外，队员在下列情况下不需要裁判员许可即可离开场地：

- 作为比赛中移动的一部分离开场地但又立即返回，如踢球时或带球过对手时使自己处于有利位置。但是，不允许离开场地后以任何欺骗对手为目的绕过任一球门重新进入场地。如果违犯，在不能掌握有利时则停止比赛。如果裁判员停止比赛，则必须在比赛停止时球所在地点以间接任意球重新开始比赛（参见规则第十三章—任意球的位置）。队员未经裁判员允许擅自离开场地将被警告。
- 由于受伤。如果队员未被替换，他需要裁判员或第三裁判员的允许方可重新进入场地。如果该队员受伤流血，在其重新进入场地前必须止住流血，并经裁判员或第三裁判员检查认可。
- 调整或束好装备。如果队员未被替换，经裁判员允许可重新进入场地。裁判员或第三裁判员在该队员重新进入场地前必须检查其装备。

Unauthorised departure from the pitch

If a player leaves the pitch without the referees' permission and for reasons not permitted in the Futsal Laws of the Game, the timekeeper or the third referee sounds the acoustic signal to inform the referees if the advantage cannot be applied. If it is necessary to stop play, the referees sanction the offending player's team with an indirect free kick from the position of the ball when the infringement was committed (see Law 13 – Position of free kick). If the advantage is applied, they must sound the acoustic signal at the next stoppage in play. The player is cautioned for deliberately leaving the pitch without the referees' permission.

Minimum number of players

Although a match may not start if either team consists of fewer than three players, the minimum number of players, including players and substitutes, required for a match is left to the discretion of member associations.

非法离开比赛场地

队员未经裁判员允许离开场地而违反竞赛规则，如果不能掌握有利，计时员或第三裁判员则以声音信号通知裁判员。如果有必要停止比赛，裁判员判罚由对方球队在犯规时球所在地点以间接任意球重新开始比赛（参见规则第十三章—任意球的位置）。如果掌握有利，则必须在下一次比赛停止时给予声音信号。队员未经裁判员允许故意离开场地将被警告。

最少队员人数

尽管任一球队的人数少于3人比赛不能开始，但一场比赛中最少的队员人数，包括队员和替补队员人数，由各会员协会自行决定。

A match may not continue if there are fewer than three players in either of the teams.

If a team has fewer than three players because one or more players has deliberately left the pitch, the referees are not obliged to stop the match immediately and the advantage may be applied. In such cases, the referees must not restart the match after play has been stopped if a team does not have the minimum number of three players.

Injured players

If there are injured players, the referees must adhere to the following guidelines:

- Allow the match to continue until the ball goes out of play if a player is, in the opinion of the referees, only slightly injured
- Play is stopped if, in the opinion of the referees, a player is seriously injured
- After questioning the injured player, the referees may authorise one, or at most two doctors, to enter the pitch to assess the injury and arrange the player's safe and swift removal from the pitch
- Stretcher-bearers should only enter the pitch with a stretcher following a signal from the referee at the same time as the doctors in order to hasten the player's removal from the pitch
- The referees must ensure that the injured player is carried off the pitch safely and swiftly
- A player is not allowed to receive treatment on the pitch, unless the seriousness of the injury requires it

任何一支球队的场上队员人数少于3人，比赛将不能继续。

如果某队因一名或多名队员故意离场而使场上少于3人，裁判员可掌握有利而无须立即停止比赛。在此情况下，在比赛停止后如果任一球队场上队员人数不足3人，裁判员不必再重新开始比赛。

受伤队员

如果有队员受伤，裁判员必须遵循以下条款：

- 如果裁判员认为队员只是受轻伤，则允许比赛继续直到比赛停止。
- 如果裁判员认为队员受伤严重，则应停止比赛。
- 在当询问受伤队员后，裁判员可允许一名或至多不超过两名医生进场察看伤情，并安排队员安全、迅速地离开场地。
- 只有当裁判员示意后，担架手才允许抬担架与队医同时入场，以加快队员离场速度。
- 裁判员应确保受伤队员安全、平稳地离开场地。
- 除非严重受伤，否则队员不允许在场上接受治疗。

- Any player bleeding from a wound must leave the pitch and may not return until the referees are satisfied that the bleeding has stopped (the third referee may check this, but the referees must authorise his entry, if he has not been substituted). A player is not allowed to wear clothing with blood on it
- As soon as the referees have authorised the doctors to enter the pitch, the player must leave the pitch, either on a stretcher or on foot. If a player does not comply, he must be cautioned for delaying the restart of play. Play is not restarted until said player has left the pitch
- An injured player may leave the pitch from a place other than the substitution zone. He may do so from any line that marks the pitch boundaries
- An injured player may be substituted, but the substitute must enter via the substitution zone once the injured player has left the pitch
- If he has not been substituted, a player who was injured may return to the pitch only after the match has restarted
- If he has not been substituted, an injured player may re-enter the pitch when the ball is in play, but only from the touch line. When the ball is out of play, he may enter the pitch from any boundary line (goal line and touch line)
- Only the referees may allow an injured player who has not been substituted to return to the pitch, whether the ball is in play or not. He is not permitted to enter if the ball is in play and if play is developing through the area in which he is located
- The referees may give permission for an injured player to return to the pitch if the third referee verifies that the player is ready

- 任何因受伤而流血的队员必须离开场地，直到裁判员认为流血被止住（第三裁判员可以检查，如果该队员没有被替换，只有裁判员有权允许其进入场地）。队员不能穿带血渍的衣服上场。
- 一旦裁判员允许医生进入场地，则受伤队员必须离开场地，无论是坐担架离场还是走出场地。如果一队员没有遵守上述规定，他将因延误比赛重新开始而被警告。只有当上述队员离开场地后比赛才能重新开始。
- 受伤队员不需要从替换区离场，他可以从场地的任何边界线处离场。
- 受伤队员可被替换，但是替补队员必须在受伤队员已经离场后从本方的替换区进场。
- 如果队员受伤没有被替换，该队员可回到比赛场地，但必须是比赛重新开始之后。
- 如果队员受伤没有被替换，该队员可在比赛进行中重新进入场地，但只能从边线处进入。如果比赛停止，他可从任何边界线（球门线和边线）入场。
- 只有裁判员有权允许没有被替换的受伤队员回到场地上，无论在比赛进行中或比赛停止时。如果比赛正在该受伤队员所在区域发展，则该队员不允许此时进入场地。
- 经第三裁判员检查核实受伤队员准备就绪，裁判员可允许该队员返回场地。

- If play has not otherwise been stopped for another reason, or if an injury suffered by a player is not the result of an infringement of the Futsal Laws of the Game, the referees must stop play and restart it with a dropped ball from the position of the ball when play was stopped, unless play was stopped inside the penalty area, in which case one of the referees drops the ball on the penalty area line at the point nearest to where the ball was located when play was stopped
- Once the referees have decided to issue a card to a player who is injured and has to leave the pitch for treatment, the referees must issue the card before the player leaves the pitch
- They do not issue a card to an injured player when he is receiving treatment, but once he has returned and before play has been restarted. If the player has to leave the pitch on a stretcher, they issue the card before he leaves the pitch
- The third referee assists the referees with the enforcement of permissions to enter the pitch granted to substitutes replacing injured players or players who were injured

Exceptions to this ruling are to be made only when:

- a goalkeeper is injured
- a goalkeeper and any other player have collided and need immediate attention
- players from the same team have collided and need immediate attention
- a serious injury has occurred, e.g. swallowed tongue, concussion, broken leg, broken arm, etc.

- 如果比赛没有因其他原因停止，或如果队员的受伤不是由于违反室内五人制足球竞赛规则所致，则裁判员必须停止比赛并在比赛停止时球所在地点以坠球重新开始比赛，除非比赛停止时球在罚球区内，在此情况下则由其中一名裁判员在比赛停止时距球所处地点最近的罚球区线上坠球重新开始比赛。
- 一旦裁判员已经决定对一受伤离场并需治疗的队员出示红牌或黄牌，则裁判员必须在该队员离场前出示。
- 裁判员不能在受伤队员接受治疗时出示红牌或黄牌，而是应在其治疗后、比赛重新开始前出示。如果该队员被担架抬离出场，应在其离场前给予。
- 第三裁判员协助裁判员，对允许替换受伤队员的替补队员或受伤队员进入场地进行监控和管理。

对本规定的例外情况仅有：

- 守门员受伤。
- 守门员和场上任何队员发生冲突需要立刻处置时。
- 当同队队员发生冲突需要立刻处置时。
- 发生严重受伤时，如吞咽舌头、脑震荡或腿、手臂骨折等。

Refreshments

The referees allow players to take refreshments during time-outs or during a stoppage in the match, but only outside the pitch, so that it does not become wet. It is not permitted to throw bags containing liquids or any other receptacle containing liquid on to the pitch.

Players sent off

- If a player who commits an infringement is sent off for a second caution or directly after the advantage has been applied and his team concedes a goal after the application of the advantage before he is sent off, the number of players in his team is not reduced, as the infringement was committed before the goal was scored
- if, during the interval or before the start of one of the periods of extra time, a player commits a sending-off offence, his team starts the next half or period of extra time with one player fewer

饮水

在比赛暂停或停止时，裁判员应允许队员补充水分，但只能在场地外，以防止场地变湿。不允许将含有液体的水袋或任何其他包含液体的容器扔进场内。

被罚令出场的队员

- 如果一队员在裁判员掌握有利后犯有第二次被警告或直接罚令出场的犯规，而其所在球队在裁判员掌握有利后、该队员被罚令出场前被进球，则他所在球队的队员人数不应被减少，这是因为犯规发生在进球前。
- 如果在中场休息期间或加时赛任一半场开始前，一队员犯有可被罚令出场的犯规，则其所在球队在下半时或加时赛各半场开始时场上少1人。

Basic equipment

Colours:

- If the jerseys of the two goalkeepers are the same colour and neither has another jersey to change into, the referee allows play to begin

If a player loses his footwear accidentally and immediately plays the ball and scores a goal, there is no infringement and the goal is awarded because he lost his footwear by accident.

Other equipment

A player may use equipment other than the basic equipment, provided that its sole purpose is to protect him physically and it poses no danger to him or any other player.

All items of clothing or equipment must be inspected by the referees and determined not to be dangerous.

Modern protective equipment, such as headgear, facemasks and knee and arm protectors made of soft, lightweight padded material are not considered dangerous and are therefore permitted.

基本装备

颜色：

- 如果双方守门员的上衣颜色相同且无其他上衣可换，裁判员可允许比赛开始。

如果一名队员意外掉了鞋子并随即在比赛中打进一球，则进球有效，因为该队员是意外掉了鞋子，并未违规。

其他装备

队员可以使用基本装备以外的其他装备，只要该装备的目的是保护自身，而且对其他队员不构成危险。

所有着装或装备必须由裁判员检查并确定无危险性。

现代防护器材，如由软质或轻便材质制成的头套、面具、护膝、护臂等不会造成危险，应允许使用。

When head covers are worn, they must:

- be black or of the same colour as the main colour of the shirt (provided players of the same team wear the same colour)
- be in keeping with the professional appearance of the player's equipment
- not be attached to the jersey
- not pose any danger to the player wearing it or any other player (e.g. opening/closing mechanism around neck)
- not have any part(s) extending out from the surface (protruding elements)

Sports spectacles are permitted if they pose no danger to the players.

If an item of clothing or equipment that has been inspected at the start of a match and determined not to be dangerous becomes dangerous or is used in a dangerous manner during the match, its use must no longer be allowed.

The use of elctronic communication systems between players and/or technical staff is not permitted.

Jewellery

All items of jewellery (necklaces, rings, bracelets, earrings, leather bands, rubber bands, etc.) are strictly forbidden and must be removed by the players and substitutes before the start of the match. Using tape to cover jewellery is not acceptable

若需使用头套，它们必须：

- 是黑色，或与运动上衣主色相同（除非同队队员身着相同颜色）。
- 同队员装备一样保持专业性外观。
- 与运动上衣分离。
- 不会给佩戴它的队员或其他队员带来危险（例如在颈部周围的锁扣装置）。
- 不具有任何部分高出表面（凸起部分）。

允许佩戴运动眼镜，只要其不对其他队员造成危险。

如果赛前已被检查并确定不具危险性的着装或装备在比赛期间变得危险或被以危险的方式使用，则不应再被允许使用。

队员和（或）球队官员之间不允许使用电子通讯系统。

饰物

比赛中严禁佩戴任何种类的珠宝饰物（项链、戒指、手镯、耳环、皮革带、橡胶带等），队员和替补队员必须在比赛开始前去除。不能用绑带包裹饰物。

Referees and assistant referees are also prohibited from wearing jewellery (except for the referee, who is permitted to wear a watch or similar device to time the match if the timekeeper is absent).

Numbering of the players

The competition rules must stipulate the numbering of the players, which is normally from 1 to 15, with number 1 reserved for a goalkeeper.

The organisers must bear in mind that it is impossible for referees to signal numbers greater than 15.

The number of each player must be visible on his back and be distinguishable from the main colour of the shirt. The competition rules must determine the size of the numbers and whether they are mandatory, as well as their size on other items of the players' basic equipment.

Disciplinary sanctions

Before the match begins, players and substitutes must be checked to ensure that they are not wearing any unauthorised clothing or jewellery. The third referee makes a second visual check of the substitutes before they enter the pitch. If a player is discovered to be wearing unauthorised clothing or jewellery during play, the referees must:

裁判员和助理裁判员也禁止佩戴任何饰物（在没有计时员时裁判员被允许佩戴手表或类似计时器计时除外）。

队员号码

竞赛规程应设定队员号码编制规则，通常是1～15号，其中1号预留给守门员。

比赛组织者应清楚对于裁判员来说不可能示意大于15的队员号码。

每个队员的号码应清晰地印在背部，并区别于球衣主色。竞赛规程应明确号码的尺寸，以及该尺寸是否为强制性规定，并规定在其他基本装备上的号码尺寸。

纪律处罚

比赛开始前，队员和替补队员必须接受检查从而确保没有穿戴任何未经允许的服装和饰物。第三裁判员应在替补队员替换上场前再次检查。如果比赛中有队员被发现穿戴未经许可的服装或饰物，则裁判员必须：

- inform the player that the item in question must be removed
- order the player to leave the pitch at the next stoppage if he is unable or unwilling to comply
- caution the player if he wilfully refuses to comply or, having been told to remove the item, is discovered to be wearing the item again

If play is stopped to caution the player, an indirect free kick must be awarded to the opposing team from the position of the ball when play was stopped (see Law 13 – Position of free kick).

Powers and duties

Futsal is a competitive sport, and referees must understand that physical contact between the players is normal and an acceptable part of the game. Nevertheless, if the players do not respect the Futsal Laws of the Game and the principles of sportsmanship, i.e. fair play, the referees must take the appropriate action to ensure that they are respected.

The referees must suspend the match if, in their opinion, the lighting is inadequate due to a failure of some kind. If the failure cannot be repaired, the referee abandons the match.

- 告知该队员违规的饰物必须被移除。
- 如果队员不能或不情愿服从，则令该队员在下一次比赛停止时离场。
- 如果队员拒绝服从，或在被告知移除穿戴物之后再次被发现穿戴该饰物，则应警告该队员。

如果比赛因警告该队员而停止，则由对方球队在比赛停止时球所在地点踢间接任意球重新开始比赛（参见规则第十三章—任意球的位置）。

权限和职责

室内五人制足球是一项竞技运动，裁判员必须理解队员之间的身体接触是正常的，并且是比赛的一部分。但是，如果队员不尊重室内五人制足球竞赛规则，例如公平竞赛等体育道德原则，则裁判员必须采取相应的行动确保规则得到尊重。

如果裁判员认为，由于一些照明灯光失灵而造成光线不足，则必须推迟比赛。如果灯光设备不能被修复，裁判员则终止比赛。

If an object thrown by a spectator hits a match official, a player or a team official, the referee may allow the match to continue, suspend play or abandon the match, depending on the severity of the incident. He must, in all cases, report the incident(s) to the appropriate authorities.

The referees have the power to caution or send off players during the half-time interval and after the match has finished as well as during extra time and kicks from the penalty mark, since disciplinary decisions remain under their jurisdiction at these times.

If one of the referees is temporarily incapacitated for any reason, play may continue under the supervision of the other referee and the assistant referees until the ball next goes out of play.

Advantage

The referees may play advantage whenever an infringement or offence occurs and the Futsal Laws of the Game do not explicitly prohibit the advantage from being applied. For example, it is permitted at a goal clearance with attacking players inside the penalty area if the goalkeeper wishes to take the clearance quickly; however, it is not permitted when a kick-in is taken incorrectly.

如果比赛官员、队员或球队官员被观众掷出的物品击中，裁判员可根据事件的严重程度令比赛继续、推迟或终止。无论哪种情况裁判员必须对所发生的事件向主办机构报告。

在中场休息、比赛刚结束，或在加时赛期间及踢球点球决胜过程中，裁判员有权警告队员或将其罚令出场，因为上述时间仍处于裁判员纪律处罚权限范围内。

如果其中一名裁判员由于任何原因不能执法，比赛则在场上另一裁判员和助理裁判员的监督下继续进行，直到比赛停止。

有利

在违规和犯规发生时裁判员可掌握有利条款。室内五人制足球竞赛规则没有明确禁止掌握有利。例如，手掷球门球时如果守门员希望快速将球开出，则允许对方队员在本方罚球区内。然而，当踢界外球违规时不应掌握有利。

The advantage is not permitted for infringements of the four-second rule, unless the infringement is committed by the goalkeeper in controlling the ball when it is already in play in his own half of the pitch, and if he loses possession of the ball. In the remaining cases: free kicks, kick-ins, goal clearances and corner kicks, the referees cannot apply the advantage.

The referees should consider the following circumstances in deciding whether to apply the advantage or stop play:

- The severity of the offence: if the infringement warrants an expulsion, the referees must stop play and send off the player unless there is an opportunity to score a goal
- The position where the offence was committed: the closer to the opposing goal, the more effective it can be
- The chances of an immediate, promising attack
- The infringement committed must not be a team' s sixth or greater accumulated foul, unless there is an opportunity to score a goal
- The atmosphere of the match

The decision to penalise the original offence must be taken within a few seconds, but it is not possible to go back if the corresponding signal has not previously been given or a new passage of play has been allowed.

违犯4秒规则不掌握有利，除非在比赛进行中，守门员在本方半场控球时，突然对球失去控制权。除此之外的任意球、踢界外球、掷球门球和角球都不应掌握有利。

裁判员应考虑以下情况以决定是掌握有利还是停止比赛：

- 犯规的严重性：如果违规行为涉及罚令出场，则裁判员必须停止比赛并将该队员罚令出场，除非存在明显的进球得分机会。
- 发生犯规的地点：越接近对方球门，掌握有利越有效。
- 有即刻、潜在的进攻机会。
- 犯规不应是某队第6次起的累计犯规，除非存在明显得分机会。
- 比赛的气氛。

判罚最初的犯规应在接下来的几秒钟内完成，但如果先前没有给出相应手势信号，或者比赛已经发展，则不能重新判罚原来的犯规。

If the offence warrants a caution, it must be issued at the next stoppage. However, unless there is a clear advantage, it is recommended that the referees stop play and caution the player immediately. If the caution is not issued at the next stoppage, it cannot be shown later.

If an infringement requires play to be restarted with an indirect free kick, the referees must apply the advantage to ensure that play flows, provided that this does not lead to any retaliation and is not prejudicial to the team against which the offence was committed.

More than one offence occurring at the same time

- Offences committed by two or more players from the same team:
  - The referees must punish the most serious offence
  - Play must be restarted according to the most serious offence committed
  - Notwithstanding the above two paragraphs, the referees caution or send off the players in accordance with the infringements committed or do not take any disciplinary action
  - If the offences committed are punishable by a direct free kick, the referees order the corresponding accumulated fouls to be recorded

如果犯规属于可警告的犯规，则警告必须在下一次比赛停止时进行。然而，除非是明显的有利情况，建议裁判员立即停止比赛并警告该队员。如果没有在下一次比赛停止时进行警告，则在此之后不能再进行警告。

如果违规行为需要以间接任意球重新开始比赛，只要不会导致任何报复或使犯规队获利，则裁判员必须掌握有利，以保证比赛的流畅。

同时发生一个以上的犯规

- 同队两名及以上队员犯规：
- – 裁判员判罚最严重的犯规。
- – 必须根据最严重的犯规重新开始比赛。
- – 尽管如此，裁判员还是要根据犯规情况进行警告、罚令出场或不进行任何纪律制裁。
- – 如果犯规为可判直接任意球的犯规，则裁判员记录相应的累计犯规次数。

- Offences committed by players from different teams:
  - The referees stop the match, as they cannot apply the advantage, and restart play with a dropped ball from the position of the ball when play was stopped, unless play was stopped inside the penalty area, in which case one of the referees drops the ball on the penalty area line at the point nearest to where the ball was located when play was stopped
  - Notwithstanding the above paragraph, the referees caution or send off the players in accordance with the infringements committed or do not take any disciplinary action
  - If the offences committed are punishable by a direct free kick, the referees order the corresponding accumulated fouls to be recorded

External interference

The referees stop play if a spectator blows a whistle and they consider that this action interferes with play, e.g. if a player picks up the ball with his hands. If play is stopped, it must be restarted with a dropped ball from the position of the ball when play was stopped, unless play was stopped inside the penalty area, in which case one of the referees drops the ball on the penalty area line at the point nearest to where the ball was located when play was stopped.

- 双方队员同时犯规：
  - 由于不能掌握有利，裁判员停止比赛，在比赛停止时球所在地点以坠球重新开始比赛，除非比赛停止时球在罚球区内，在此情况下则应由其中一名裁判员在比赛停止时距球所处地点最近的罚球区线上坠球重新开始比赛。
  - 尽管如此，裁判员还是要根据犯规情况进行警告、罚令出场或不进行任何纪律制裁。
  - 如果犯规为可判直接任意球的犯规，则裁判员记录相应的累计犯规次数。

外部干扰

如果一观众鸣哨，裁判员认为此行为干扰了比赛，例如队员因此用手捡起球，则应令比赛停止。如果比赛停止，则应在比赛停止时球所在地点以坠球重新开始比赛，除非比赛停止时球在罚球区内，在此情况下则应由其中一名裁判员在比赛停止时距球所处地点最近的罚球区线上坠球重新开始比赛。

Four-second count when the ball is in play

Each time that a team's goalkeeper is in possession of the ball while it is in play and in his own half of the pitch, one of the referees must visibly perform the four-second count.

Restart of play

The referees especially ensure that restarts of play are carried out quickly and do not allow play not to be restarted immediately for tactical reasons after a temporary stoppage (kick-in, goal clearance, corner kick or free kick). In these cases, the four-second count starts and it is not necessary to use the whistle. In cases where the restart does not allow the four-second count (kick-off or penalty kick), the player or players who delay it are cautioned.

Persons holding balls are permitted to position themselves around the pitch to facilitate restarts and the development of play.

比赛进行中4秒计时

比赛进行中，每当一队的守门员在本方半场内控制球，其中一名裁判员必须用可见的方式示意4秒计时。

比赛重新开始

裁判员应特别注意确保尽快重新开始比赛，不能允许比赛在短暂停止（踢界外球、掷球门球、角球或任意球）后由于战术原因不能立即重新开始。在此情况下，应开始4秒计时，且不需使用哨音。在不需要进行4秒计时情况下（比赛开球、罚球点球）重新开始比赛时，一名或多名队员延误比赛重新开始将被警告。

允许持球人在场边范围选位以便使比赛重新开始和进行。

Positioning with ball in play

Recommendations

- The play should be between the referee and the second referee
- The referees should use a wide diagonal system
- Staying outside and parallel to the touch line makes it easier to keep the play and the other referee within the referee's field of vision
- The referee nearest to the play should be within the other referee's field of vision
- One of the referees should be close enough to see play without interfering with it
- The referees only enter the pitch to obtain a better view of the play
- "What needs to be seen" is not always in the vicinity of the ball. The referees should also pay attention to:
  - aggressive individual player confrontations off the ball
  - possible offences in the penalty area towards which play is heading
  - offences occurring after the ball is played away

General positioning during the match

One of the referees must be in line with the second-last member of the defednding team or the ball if it is nearer the goal line than the second-last member of the defednding team. The referees must always face the pitch.

比赛中选位

建议：

- 比赛应在裁判员及第二裁判员所在位置之间进行。
- 裁判员应采用大对角线跑位方式选位。
- 保持在边线外并且身体与边线平行，以便使比赛和另一裁判员均在视线范围内。
- 离比赛较近的裁判员应在另一裁判员的视线范围内。
- 其中一名裁判员在不干扰比赛的情况下，应尽量靠近以便观察。
- 仅在需要获得更好观察位置时，裁判员才进入场地。
- “需要被看到的情况”并总是发生在球附近。裁判员应注意：
  - 个别无球队员具有攻击性的行为。
  - 可能在比赛发展方向罚球区内发生的犯规。
  - 球被踢出后发生的犯规。

比赛期间一般选位原则

其中一名裁判员应站在与倒数第二名防守队员平齐的位置上，或者当球较倒数第二名防守队员更接近球门线时站在与球齐平的位置上。裁判员始终面向场内。

Goalkeeper releasing the ball

One of the referees must take a position in line with the edge of the penalty area and check that the goalkeeper does not touch the ball with his hands outside the penalty area, while also timing the number of seconds he is in possession of the ball.

Once the goalkeeper has released the ball, the referee must take a suitable position for controlling the match.

"Goal – no goal" situations

When a goal has been scored and there is no doubt about the decision, the referee and the second referee must make eye contact and the referee nearest to the timekeeper's table must approach the timekeeper and the third referee, to communicate the number of the player who scored the goal with the mandatory signal.

If a goal has been scored but the ball appears to still be in play, the referee who is nearest blows his whistle to attract the attention of the other referee and then the referee nearest to the timekeeper's table approaches the timekeeper and the third referee, to communicate the number of the player who scored the goal with the mandatory signal.

Positioning in ball out of play situations

The best position is one from which the referee can make the right decision. All recommendations about positioning are based on probabilities and must be adjusted using specific information about the teams, the players and events in the match up to that point.

守门员发球

其中一名裁判员必须站在齐平于罚球区上沿的边线处，以便观察守门员是否在罚球区外用手触球，同时对守门员控制球进行计时。

一旦守门员发出球后，裁判员必须选择合适的位置以便控制比赛。

“进球—非进球”情况

当发生进球且没有疑问时，裁判员和第二裁判员必须进行眼神交流，而距记录台最近的裁判员必须靠近计时台和第三裁判员，用必要的信号告知进球队员的号码。

如果进球发生但比赛看上去仍未停止，最近的裁判员鸣哨引起另一裁判员的注意，然后距记录台最近的裁判员靠近计时台和第三裁判员，用必要的信号告知进球队员的号码。

比赛停止时选位

最好的选位能使裁判员做出正确的判罚决定。所有关于选位的建议都是基于可能发生的情况，并必须根据球队、队员和比赛情况的特定信息进行调整。

The positions suggested in the following graphics are basic; some are recommended to referees and others are mandatory. The reference to a "zone" is intended to emphasise that every recommended position is actually an area within which the referee is most likely to optimise his effectiveness. The zone may be larger, smaller or differently shaped depending on circumstances.

1. Positioning – kick-off (mandatory)

At the start of the match, the referee situated on the touch line where the substitution zone is located must be in line with the halfway line to check that the kick-off is taken in accordance with the established procedure.

The second referee must be in line with the second-last defender of the team that is not taking the kick-off.

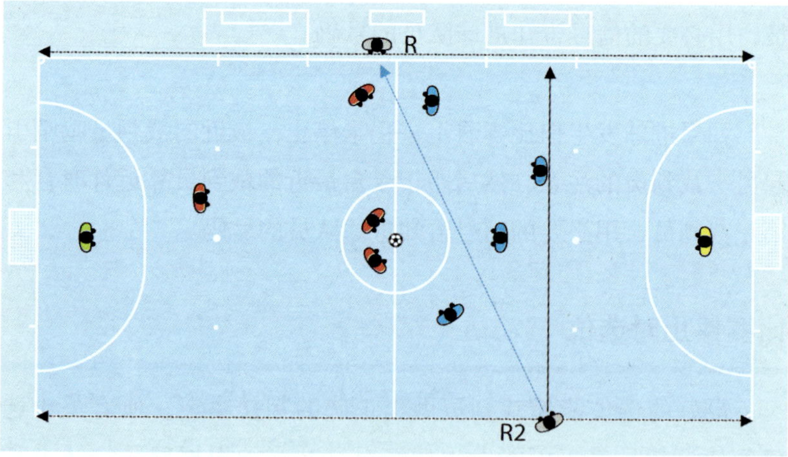

2. Positioning – goal clearance

1. One of the referees must check first if the ball is inside the penalty area:

以下图示为基本的选位方法。有些选位方法属建议性的，有些则是强制性的。图示中示意的“区域”旨在强调每个建议性的选位，实际上是最能使裁判员观察效率最佳化的区域。根据不同的情况，这个区域可能稍大也可能稍小，或形状也会有所不同。

1. 选位—开球（强制性的）

比赛开始时，裁判员站在替补席一侧的边线上并与中线齐平，监督比赛开球按照规则规定的程序进行。

第二裁判员必须齐平于非开球队倒数第二名防守队员。

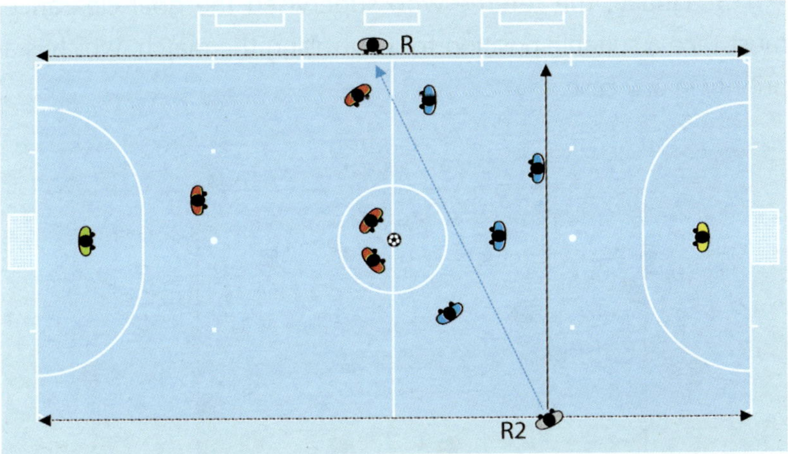

2. 选位 — 掷球门球

1. 其中一名裁判员必须查看球是否在罚球区内：

- If the ball is not placed correctly, the referee may start the four-second count if he considers that the goalkeeper was ready to take the goal clearance or is delaying picking the ball up in his hands for tactical reasons

2. Once the ball is inside the penalty area, one of the referees must take a position in line with the edge of the penalty area to check that the ball leaves the penalty area (ball in play) and that the the member of the opposing team are outside. He then performs the four-second count, irrespective of whether he has started it in accordance with the previous point.

3. Finally, the referee who supervised the goal clearance must take a suitable position for controlling the match, which is a priority in any case.

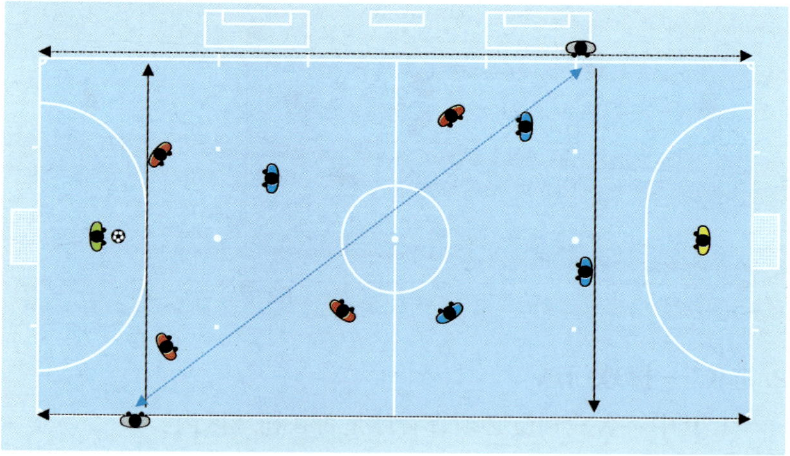

• 如果球不在罚球区内，但裁判员认为守门员已经准备好掷球或由于战术原因拖延捡球的时间，他可以开始4秒计时。

2. 一旦球在罚球区内，其中一名裁判必须站在与罚球区上沿齐平的位置，观察球是否离开罚球区（比赛开始）且对方队员是否在罚球区外。然后示意开始4秒计时，而是否开始4秒计时则要根据先前的情况。

3. 最后，观察掷球门球的裁判员必须选择一个合适的位置控制比赛，这在任何情况下都是首先要做到的。

3. Positioning – corner kick [mandatory (1)]

During a corner kick, the referee nearest to the place where it is to be taken takes a position on the touch line at a distance of approximately 5m from the corner arc. From this position he must check that the ball is properly placed inside the corner arc and that the defenders have retreated 5 m. The referee furthest from the place where the corner kick is to be taken takes a position behind the corner arc in line with the goal line. From this position he watches the ball and the behaviour of the players.

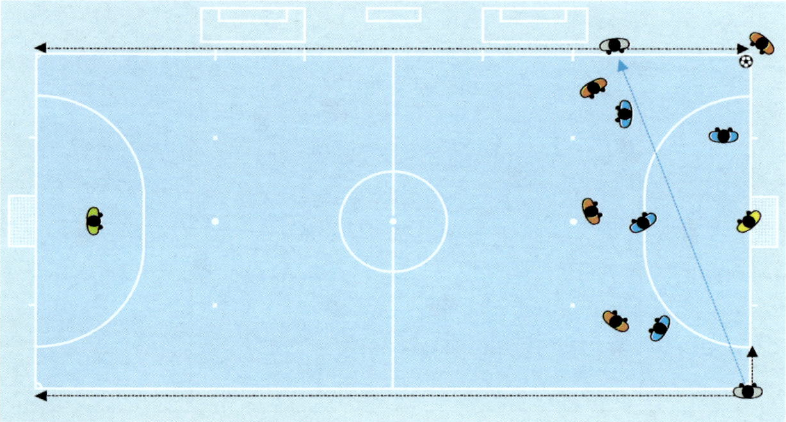

3. 选位 — 角球［强制性的（1）］

踢角球时，近端裁判员选位在距角球弧约5米的边线区域，从这个位置上查看球是否摆放在角球弧内，以及防守队员是否已经退出5米。远端裁判员位于角球弧外与球门线齐平的位置上，并从此位置上观察球和队员的行为。

4. Positioning – corner kick [mandatory (2)]

4. 选位 — 角球［强制性的（2）］

5. Positioning – free kick (1)

During a corner kick, the referee nearest to the place where it is to be taken takes a position on the touch line at a distance of approximately 5m from the corner arc. From this position he must check that the ball is properly placed inside the corner arc and that the defenders have retreated 5 m. The referee furthest from the place where the corner kick is to be taken takes a position behind the corner arc in line with the goal line. From this position he watches the ball and the behaviour of the players.

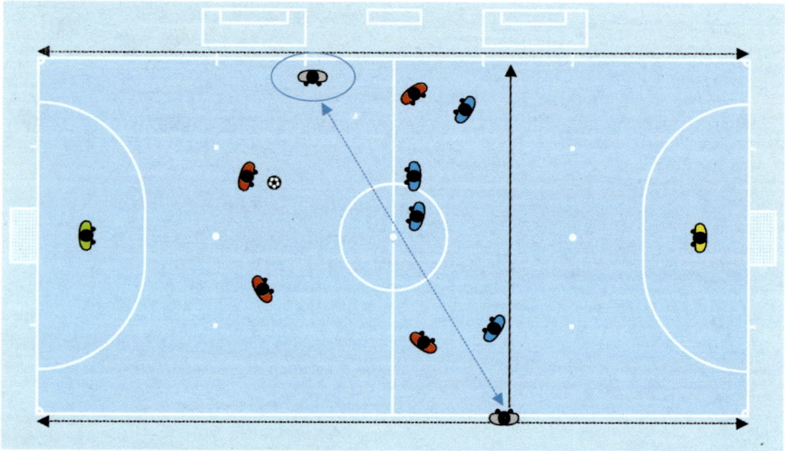

5. 选位 — 任意球（1）

罚任意球时，近端裁判员应位于与罚任意球地点齐平的位置上，观察球的摆放位置是否正确，以及球被踢出时提前进入规定距离的队员情况。远端裁判员位于与倒数第二名防守队员或球门线齐平的位置上，这在任何情况下都是首先要做到的。两名裁判员都必须时刻准备跟踪球的运行轨迹，并且当没有与球门线齐平，而一直接任意球又朝着球门方向踢出时，要沿着边线向角球区的方向跑动。

6. Positioning – free kick (2)

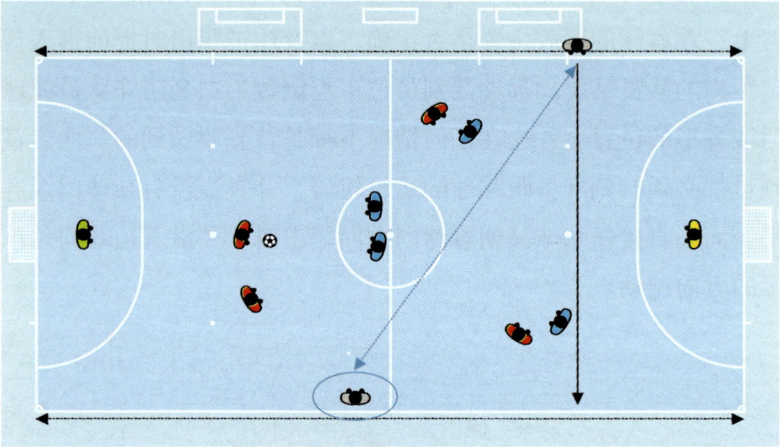

7. Positioning – free kick (3)

6. 选位 — 任意球（2）

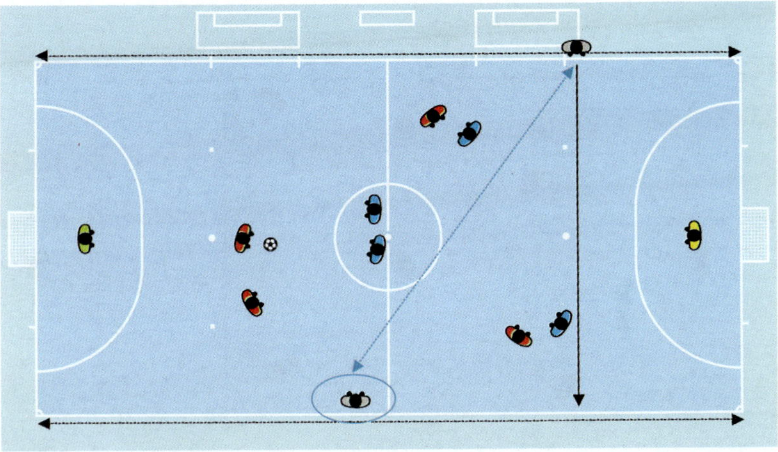

7. 选位 — 任意球（3）

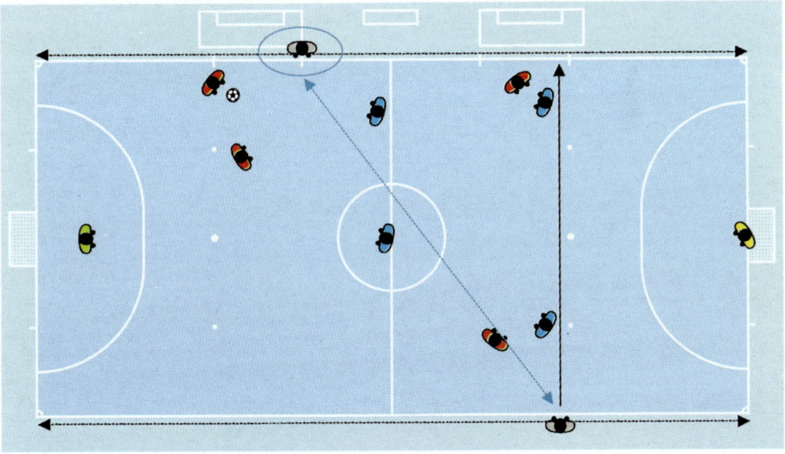

8. Positioning – free kick (4)

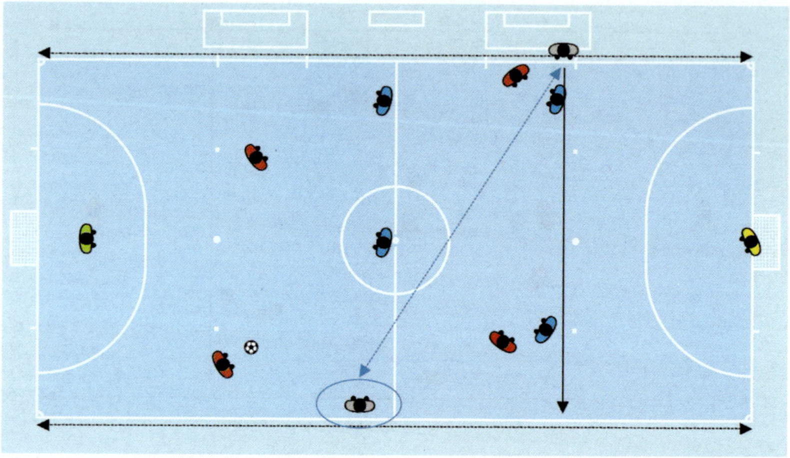

8. 选位 — 任意球（4）

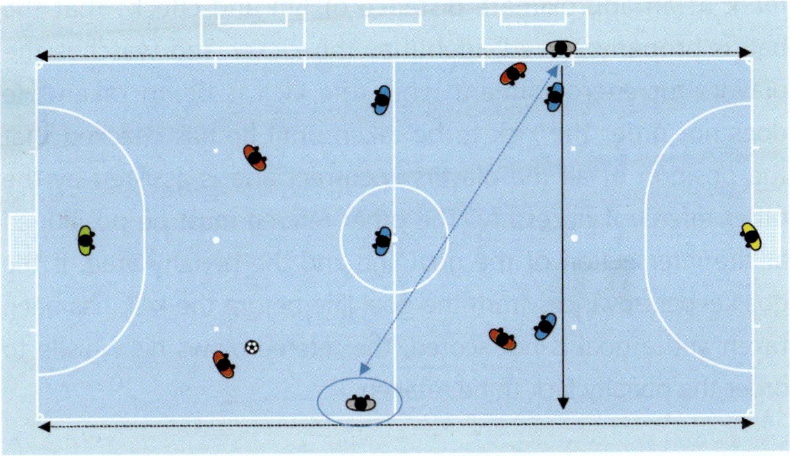

9. Positioning – penalty kick (mandatory)

One of the referees is positioned in line with the penalty mark at an approximate distance of 5m and checks that the ball is properly placed, identifies the kicker and watches the players for encroachment while the kick is being taken. He does not order the kick to be taken until he has checked that the position of all the players is correct and is assisted by the other referee if necessary. The other referee must be positioned at the intersection of the goal line and the penalty area. If the goalkeeper advances from the goal line before the kick has been taken and a goal is not scored, the referee blows his whistle to order the penalty kick to be retaken.

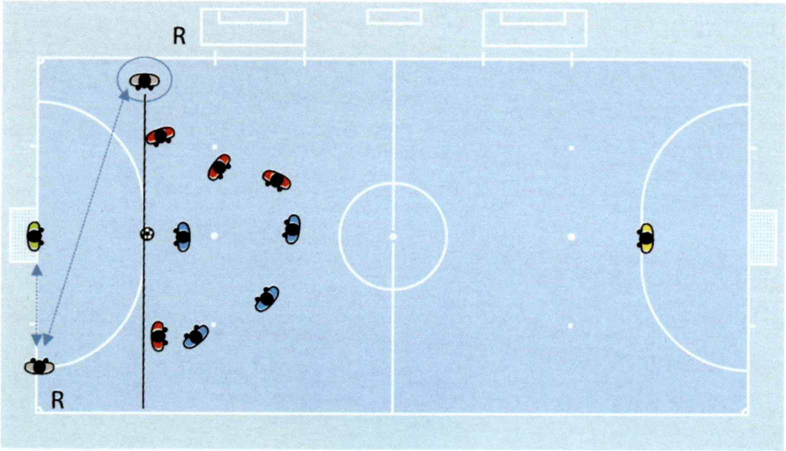

9. 选位 — 罚球点球（强制性的）

其中一名裁判员位于与罚球点齐平约5米的地点，查看球的摆放是否正确，并确定罚球队员，以及观察球被踢出时提前进入规定距离的队员情况。在确认所有队员的位置正确后给出罚球信号。如果必要，另一裁判员可协助进行。这名裁判员位于球门线与罚球区线的交点处。如果守门员在球踢出前提前从球门线上向前移动而球未踢进球门，则裁判员鸣哨示意重罚。

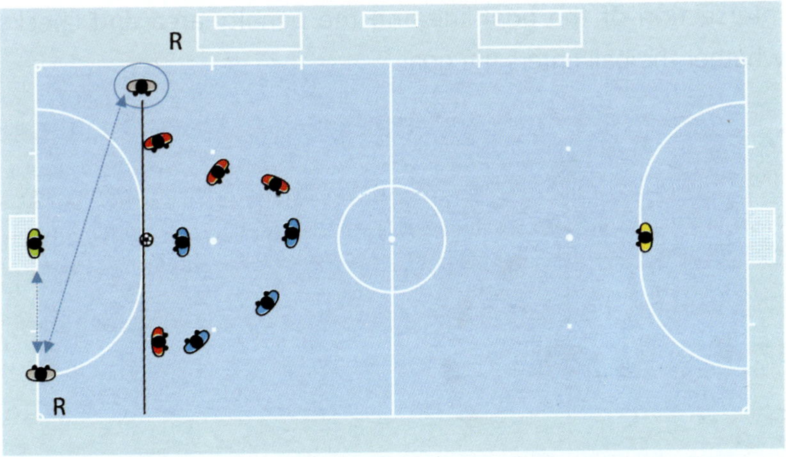

10. Positioning – kicks from the second penalty mark (mandatory)

One of the referees is positioned in line with the second penalty mark at an approximate distance of 5m and checks that the ball is properly placed, identifies the kicker and watches the players for encroachment while the kick is being taken. He does not order the kick to be taken until he has checked that the position of all the players is correct and is assisted by the other referee if necessary. The other referee must be positioned at the intersection of the goal line and the penalty area and checks whether the ball enters the goal.

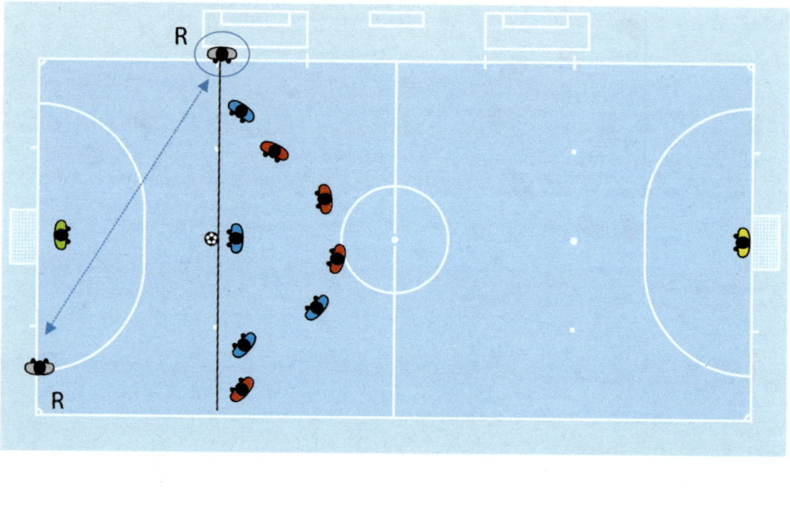

10. 选位 — 第二罚球点罚球（强制性的）

其中一名裁判员位于与第二罚球点齐平约5米的地点，查看球的摆放是否正确，并明确罚球队员，以及观察球被踢出时提前进入规定距离的队员情况。在确认所有队员的位置正确后给出罚球信号。如果必要，另一裁判员可协助进行。这名裁判员位于球门线与罚球区线的交点处，观察球是否越过球门线。

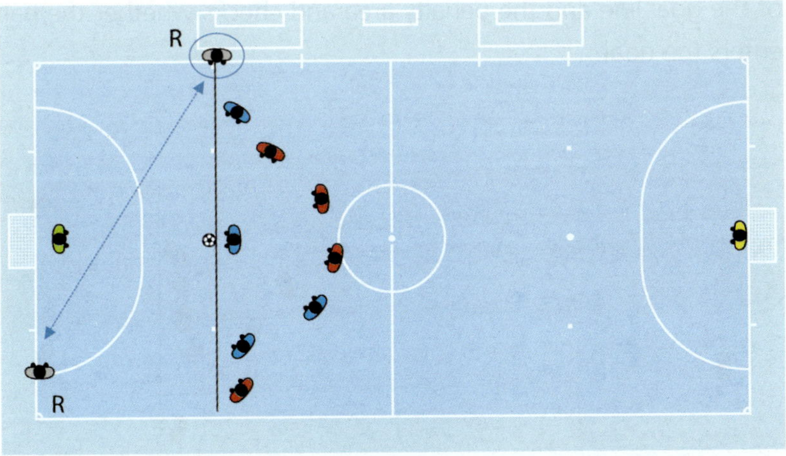

11. Positioning – free kicks beginning with the sixth accumulated foul [mandatory (1)]

One of the referees is positioned in line with the position of the ball at an approximate distance of 5 m, if possible, checks that the ball is properly placed, identifies the kicker and watches the players for encroachment while the kick is being taken. He does not order the kick to be taken until he has checked that the position of all the players is correct and is assisted by the other referee. The other referee must be positioned at the intersection of the goal line and the penalty area and checks whether the ball enters the goal.

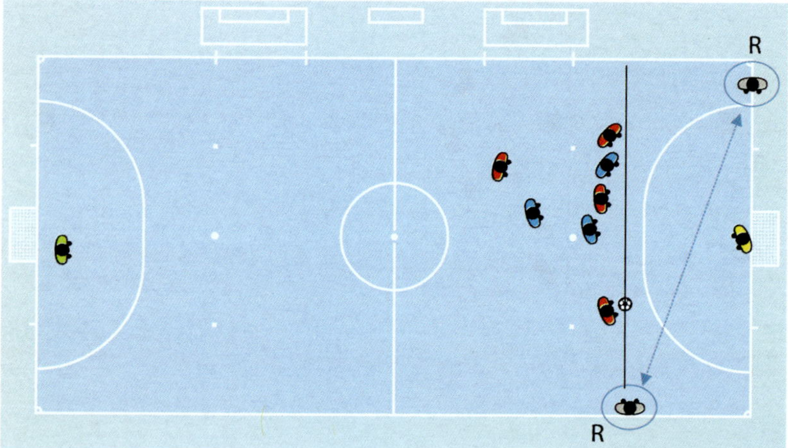

11. 选位 — 第6次累计犯规开始的任意球［强制性的（1）］

其中一名裁判员位于与球的位置齐平约5米的地点，查看球的摆放是否正确，并明确罚球队员，以及观察球被踢出时提前进入规定距离的队员情况。在确认所有队员的位置正确后给出罚球信号。如果必要，另一裁判员可协助进行。这名裁判员应位于球门线与罚球区线的交点处，观察球是否越过球门线。

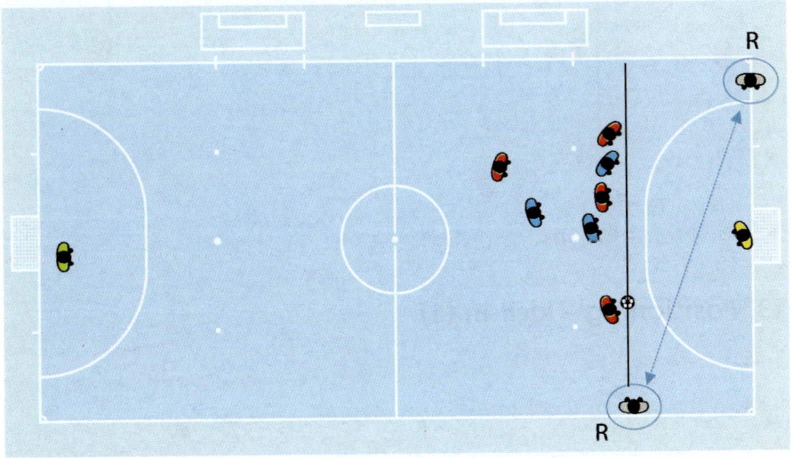

12. Positioning – free kicks beginning with the sixth accumulated foul [mandatory (2)]

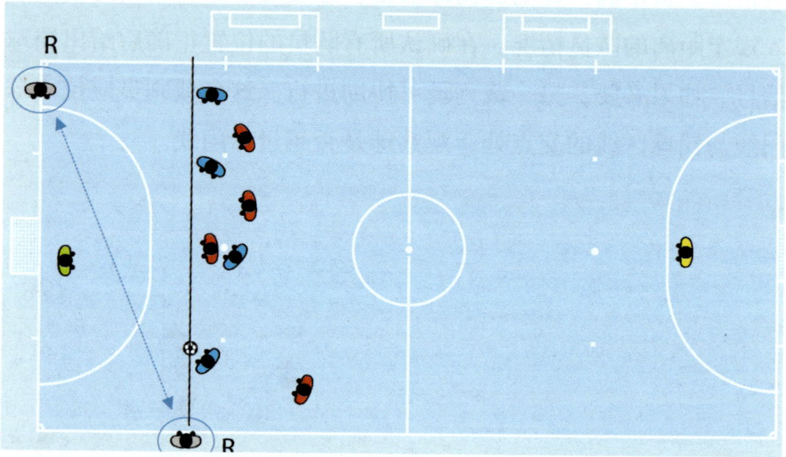

13. Positioning – kick-in (1)

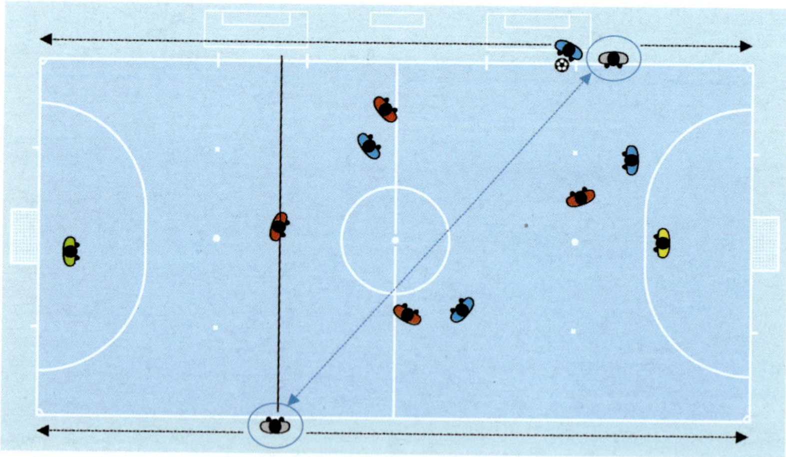

12. 选位 — 第6次累计犯规开始的任意球［强制性的（2）］

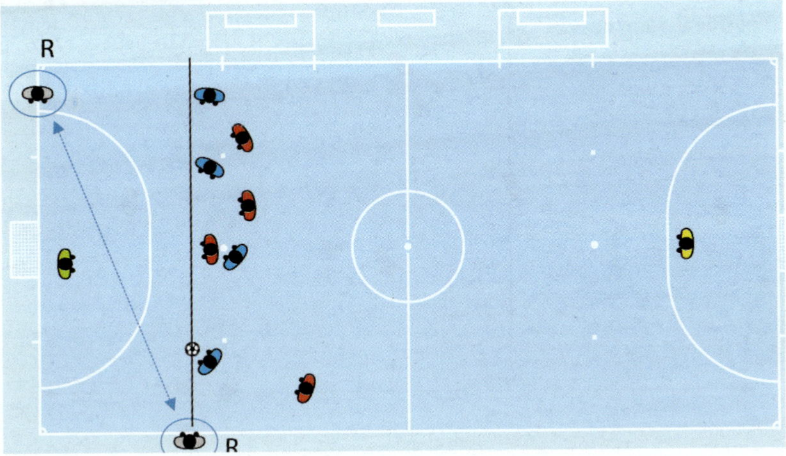

13. 选位 — 踢界外球（1）

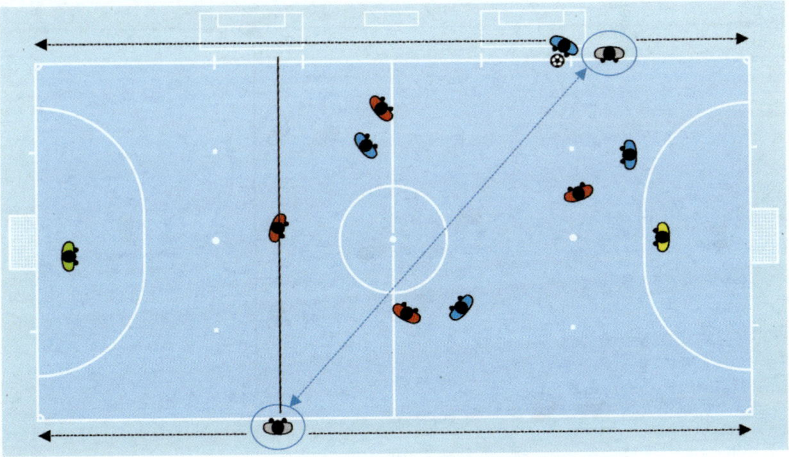

14. Positioning – kick-in (2)

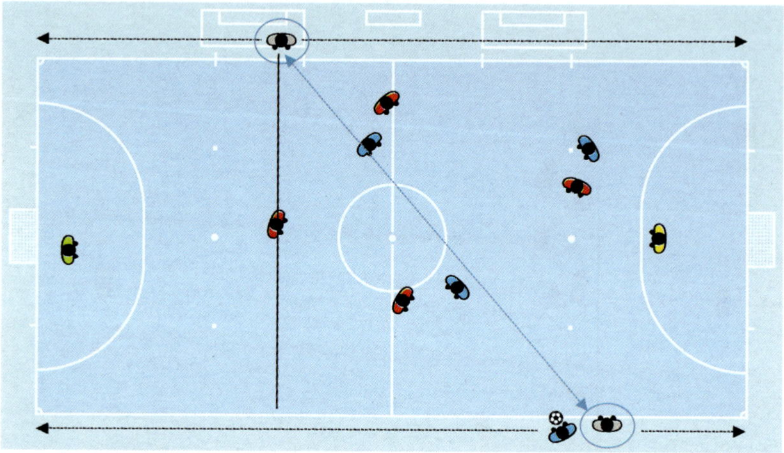

15. Positioning – kick-in (3)

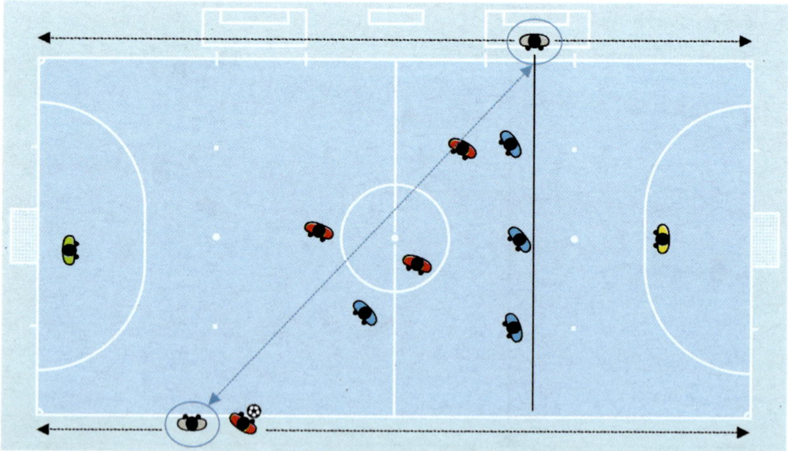

14. 选位 — 踢界外球（2）

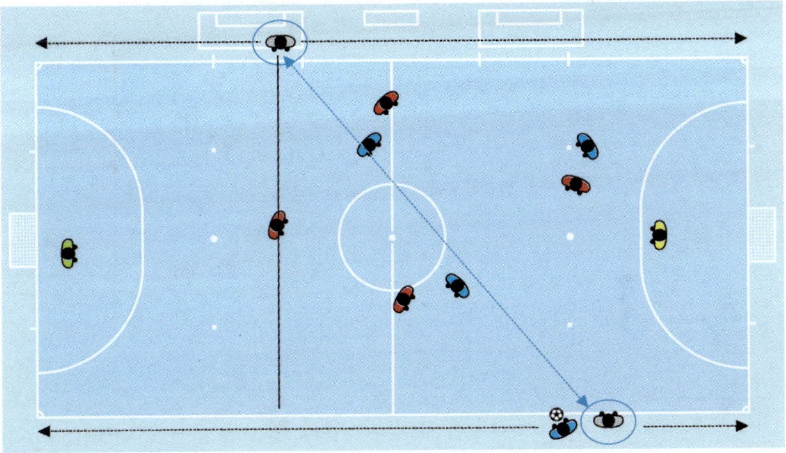

15. 选位 — 踢界外球（3）

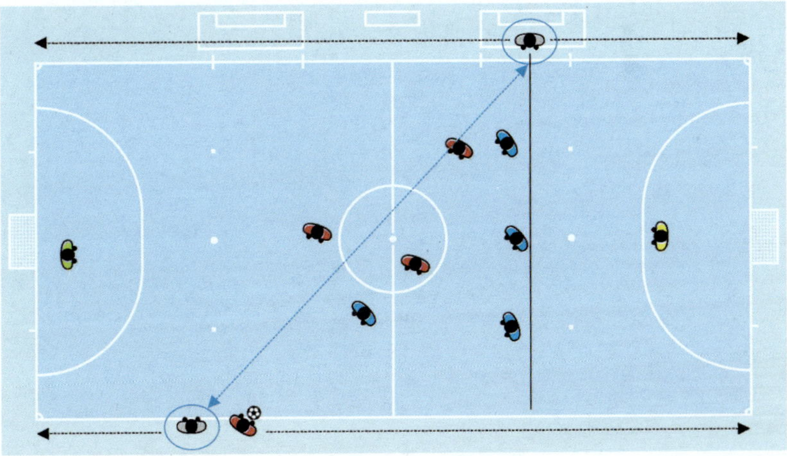

16. Positioning – kick-in (4)

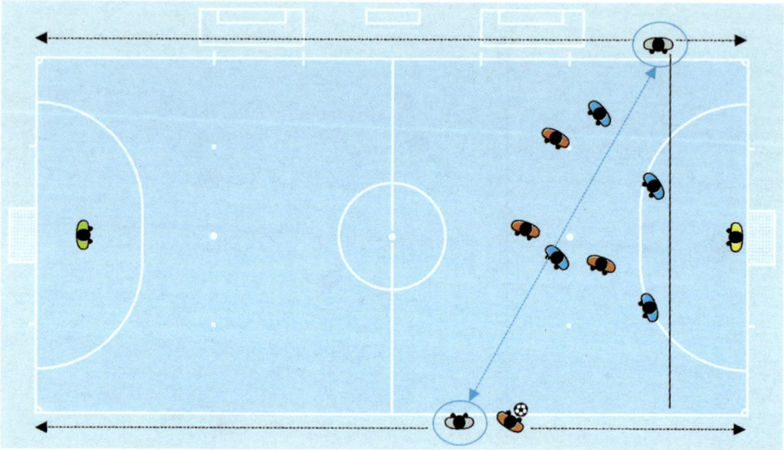

16. 选位 — 踢界外球（4）

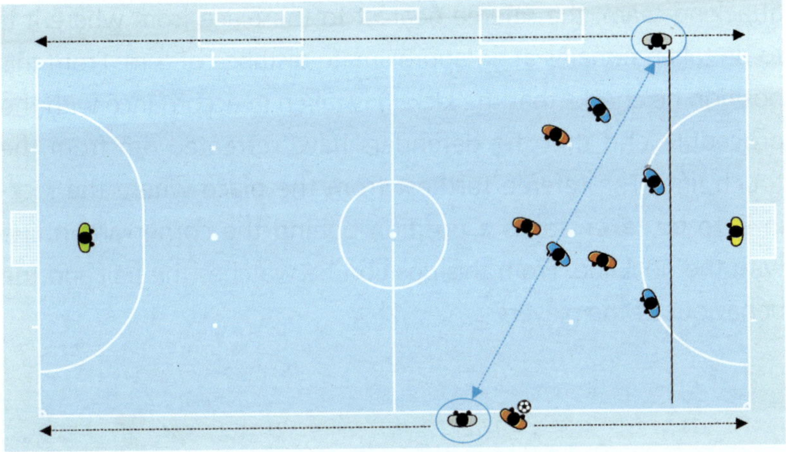

17. Positioning – kick-in [mandatory (5)]

During a kick-in close to the corner arc in favour of the attacking team, the referee nearest to the place from where it is to be taken remains at an approximate distance of 5 m. From this position he checks that the kick-in is taken in accordance with the procedure and that the defenders have retreated 5m from the touch line. The referee furthest from the place where the kick-in is to be taken takes a position behind the corner arc in line with the goal line. From this position he watches the ball and the behaviour of the players.

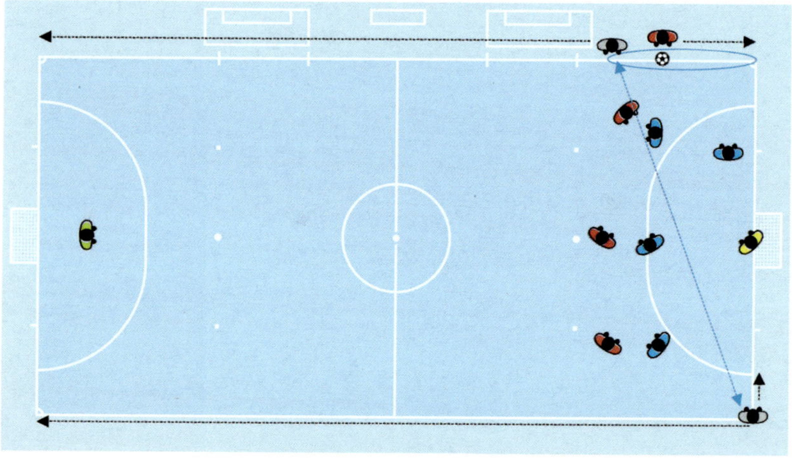

17. 选位 — 踢界外球［强制性的（5）］

攻方踢靠近角球弧的界外球时，近端裁判员位于与界外球踢出地点相距约5米的地方。从此位置上查看界外球踢出是否符合程序，以及防守队员是否已经距边线5米。远端裁判员位于角球弧后与球门线齐平的位置上，从此位置上观察球及队员的行为。

18. Positioning – kicks from the penalty mark to determine the winner of a match or home-and-away (mandatory)

His main duty is to check if the ball crosses the line and whether the goalkeeper advances from the line:

- when it is clear that the ball has crossed the goal line, the referee must make eye contact with the second referee to check that no infringement has been committed

The second referee must be situated in line with the penalty mark at an approximate distance of 3m to check that the ball and the goalkeeper of the team of the kicker are correctly positioned.

The third referee must be situated in the centre circle to control the remaining players of both teams.

The timekeeper must be positioned at the timekeeper's table and checks that the players excluded from taking the penalty kicks and the team officials behave correctly.

18. 选位 — 踢球点球决胜（强制性的）

裁判员位于距球门2米的球门线位置上。他的职责主要是查看球是否越过球门线，以及守门员是否从球门线提前向前移动：

- 当球清楚地越过球门线，则裁判员必须与第二裁判员进行眼神交流以确认无违规发生。

第二裁判员位于与罚球点齐平约3米的位置上，查看球、守门员和罚球队员的位置是否正确。

第三裁判员位于场地中圈内管理双方队员。

计时员位于计时台，确保球队不参加罚球点球的队员和官员行为恰当。

All the referees make a note of the penalty kicks taken and the numbers of the players who took them.

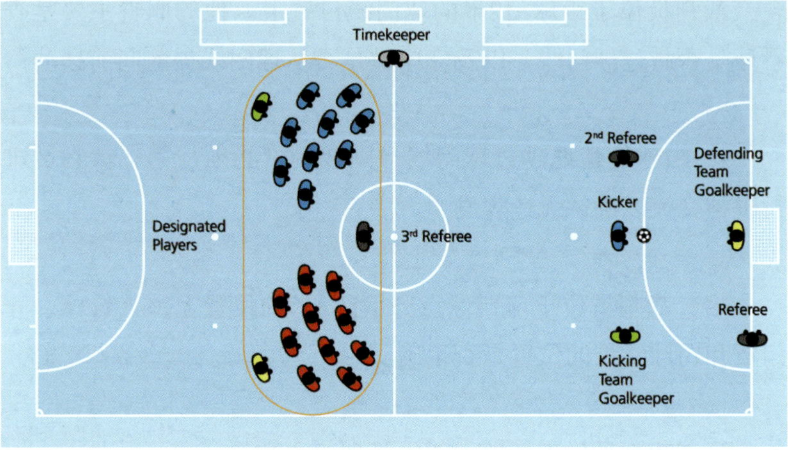

所有裁判员需记录罚球点球执行情况，以及罚球点球队员的号码。

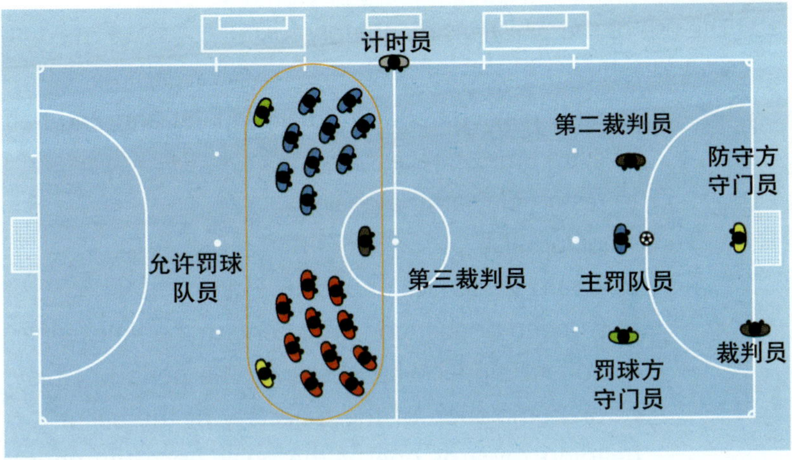

Use of whistle

The use of the whistle is mandatory for:

- kick-offs:
  - to start play (1st and 2nd half and 1st and 2nd half of extra time, if necessary)
  - to restart play after a goal
- stopping play:
  - to award a free kick or penalty kick
  - to suspend or abandon or to confirm the timekeeper's acoustic signal when he ends the period of play, or on completion of the trajectory of the ball if it is heading towards one of the goals once the period has ended
- restarting play for:
  - free kicks to ensure that the defending players observe the required distance
  - kicks from the second penalty mark
  - free kicks without a wall beginning with the sixth accumulated foul
  - penalty kicks
- restarting play after it has been stopped due to:
  - the issue of a caution or sending-off for misconduct
  - injury to one or more players

哨子的使用

必须鸣哨的情况：

- 开球：
  - 开始比赛（上、下半场以及加时赛上、下半场）。
  - 进球后重新开始比赛。
- 停止比赛：
  - 判罚任意球或球点球时。
  - 如果比赛被推迟、取消或需确认计时员半场结束时给予的声音信号，或确认在各半场结束时当球向任一球门行进时球运行结束。
- 重新开始比赛：
  - 罚任意球时需确保防守队员遵守规定的距离。
  - 第二罚球点罚球。
  - 罚第6次累计犯规开始的无人墙任意球。
  - 罚球点球。
- 由于以下原因停止比赛后重新开始比赛：
  - 对不正当行为执行警告或罚令出场。
  - 一名或多名队员受伤。

The use of the whistle is not needed to:

- stop play for:
  - a goal clearance, corner kick or kick-in (it is mandatory if the situation is unclear)
  - a goal (it is mandatory if the ball has not clearly entered the goal)
- restart play from:
  - a free kick if the distance of 5m has not been requested or the opposing team to the kicker has not committed six accumulated fouls or for a goal clearance, corner kick or kick-in

The whistle may not be used to:

- restart play with a dropped ball

A whistle which is used too frequently will have less impact when it is needed. When the team taking a free kick, kick-in or corner kick requests that the defending players observe the required distance or the correct positioning of the opposing players during a goal clearance, the referees will clearly inform the players that play cannot be restarted until after the whistle. If in these cases the player restarts play before the referees' whistle, the player is cautioned for delaying the restart of play.

If during play one of the referees sounds his whistle by mistake, the referees must stop the match if they consider this action to interfere with play. If the referees stop the match, they must restart play with a dropped ball from the position of the ball when play was stopped, unless play was stopped inside the penalty area, in which case one of the referees drops the ball on the penalty area line at the point nearest to where the ball was located when play was stopped. If the sound of the whistle does not interfere with play, the referees give clear signals to play on.

不需要鸣哨的情况：

- 由于以下原因的比赛停止：
  - 掷球门球、角球或踢界外球（情况不明时必须鸣哨）。
  - 进球（如果进球不清楚时必须鸣哨）。
- 以下情况重新开始比赛：
  - 罚任意球时未请求管理5米距离，或主罚队员的对方队累计犯规未达到6次，或掷球门球、角球、踢界外球时。

可不鸣哨的情况：

- 以坠球重新开始比赛时。

频繁使用哨音将降低哨音在需要鸣哨时的效果。当一队踢任意球、界外球或角球时，要求对方退出规定距离，或掷球门球过程中要求对方队员处于规定位置时，裁判则应清楚地告知队员，在其鸣哨前不能重新开始比赛。在此情况下，如果队员在裁判员未鸣哨前重新开始比赛，则该队员将因延误比赛重新开始而被警告。

如果比赛中一名裁判员错误鸣哨，如果他们认为这一行为干扰了比赛，则必须停止比赛。如果裁判员停止比赛，则应在比赛停止时球所在地点以坠球重新开始比赛，除非比赛停止时球在罚球区内，在此情况下则应由其中一名裁判员在比赛停止时距球所处地点最近的罚球区线上坠球重新开始比赛。如果哨音没有干扰比赛，则裁判员应给予清楚信号使比赛继续。

Body language

Body language is a tool that the referees use to:

- help themselves control the match
- show authority and self-control

Body language is not:

- a means of justifying a decision

肢体语言

肢体语言是裁判员用于表达以下行为的工具：

- 帮助自己控制比赛。
- 显示权威和自我控制。

身体语言不是：

- 解释判罚的方式。

Duties and responsibilities

The third referee and the timekeeper help the referees to control the match in accordance with the Futsal Laws of the Game. They also assist the referees in all other matters involving the running of the match at the request and under the direction of the referees. This commonly includes such matters as:

- inspecting the pitch, the balls used and players' equipment
- determining if problems with equipment or bleeding have been resolved
- monitoring the substitution procedure
- maintaining back-up records of time, goals, accumulated fouls and misconduct

Positioning of the assistant referees and teamwork

1. Kick-off

The third referee is situated at the timekeeper's table and checks that the substitutes, officials and other persons are correctly positioned.

The timekeeper is situated at the timekeeper's table and checks that the kick-off is taken correctly.

2. General positioning during the match

The third referee checks that substitutes, officials and other persons are in the correct position. To do so he may move along the touch line, if necessary, but without entering the pitch.

职责和责任

依照室内五人制足球竞赛规则，第三裁判员和计时员应帮助裁判员控制比赛，他们也应在裁判员的要求和指挥下协助处理比赛运行中所有其他事务。这些事务通常包括以下内容：

- 检查场地、比赛用球和队员装备。
- 决定装备是否有问题或确定流血已被妥善处理。
- 监督替补程序。
- 记录时间、进球、累计犯规和不正当行为。

助理裁判员的选位和团队配合

1. 开球

第三裁判员位于计时台并查看替补队员、官员及其他人员处于正确的位置上。

计时员位于计时台并查看比赛开球是否正确执行。

2. 比赛中的一般选位原则

第三裁判员查看替补队员、官员及其他人员是否处于正确的位置。如果必要，他可以沿着边线移动，但不能进入场地。

The timekeeper is positioned at the timekeeper's table and ensures that the chronometer is stopped and started in accordance with the development of play.

3. Substitutions

The third referee checks that the substitutes' equipment is correct and that the substitutions are made correctly. To do so he may move along the touch line, if necessary, but without entering the pitch.

4. Kicks from the penalty mark

The third referee must be positioned in the half of the pitch where the penalty kicks are not being taken, together with the eligible players. From this position he observes the players' behaviour and checks that no player takes another penalty kick before all of the other eligible players in his team have done so.

计时员位于计时台并确保按照比赛的进行情况开启或停止计时器。

3. 替换队员

第三裁判员要查看替补队员的装备和换人是否合乎规定。如果必要，他可以沿着边线移动，但不能进入场地。

4. 罚球点球

第三裁判员必须与其他场上合法队员一起位于非罚球点球所在的半场内，从此位置上观察队员的行为，并确保没有队员在所在球队其他所有具有罚球点球资格的队员未罚球前再次罚球。

The timekeeper is positioned at the timekeeper's table and records all the goals scored.

Assistant referee signals (mandatory)

The assistant referees must give the signals for a team's fifth accumulated foul and a request for a time-out, indicating with their arms the bench of the team that has committed its fifth accumulated foul or requested the time-out.

Acoustic signal

The acoustic signal is an essential signal in a match to be used only when necessary in order to gain the attention of the referee.

Situations when the acoustic signal is mandatory:

- End of the periods of play
- Notice of a request for a time-out
- Notice of the end of a time-out
- Communication of the fifth accumulated foul by a team
- Notice of incorrect behaviour by substitutes or team officials
- Notice of a breach of the substitution procedure
- Notice of a disciplinary error committed by the referees
- Notice of external interference

计时员在记录台位置记录所有进球情况。

助理裁判员的手势（强制性的）

助理裁判员必须在某队累计犯规达到5次和要求暂停时给予手势，以手臂朝向示意累计犯规达到5次或要求暂停的球队。

声音信号

比赛中声音信号是一种基本信号，仅用于在必要时引起裁判员的注意。

必须使用声音信号的情况：

- 每个半场比赛结束。
- 申请暂停。
- 暂停结束。
- 某队第5次累积犯规。
- 某队替补队员或官员的不恰当的行为。
- 替补程序违例。
- 裁判员在纪律制裁中出现错误。
- 场外出现的干扰。

If during the match the timekeeper sounds the acoustic signal by mistake, the referees must stop the match if they consider this action to interfere with play. If the referees stop the match, they must restart play with a dropped ball from the position of the ball when play was stopped, unless play was stopped inside the penalty area, in which case one of the referees drops the ball on the penalty area line at the point nearest to where the ball was located when play was stopped. If the sound of the acoustic signal does not interfere with play, the referees give clear signals to play on.

If a team that has committed four accumulated fouls commits another one and the referees decide to apply the advantage, the third referee places the signal for the fifth accumulated foul in the correct place on the timekeeper's table. However, if that team commits a new accumulated foul before the ball is out of play, the assistant referees must sound the acoustic signal, unless the opposing team to the one that committed the foul has an obvious goalscoring opportunity.

Chronometer

If the chronometer does not work properly, the assistant referees inform the referees of this fact. The timekeeper must continue timing the match using a manual chronometer. In such a situation, they invite an official from each team in order to inform them of the real match time.

If, after a stoppage in play, the timekeeper forgets to start the chronometer, the referees order the time that was not counted to be added on.

如果比赛中计时员发出错误的信号，而裁判员认为这一举动干扰了比赛，则必须停止比赛。如果裁判员停止比赛，则应在比赛停止时球所在地点以坠球方式重新开始比赛。除非比赛停止的地点发生在罚球区内，在此情况下应由其中一名裁判员在比赛停止时距球所处地点最近的罚球区线上坠球重新开始比赛。如果哨声没有干扰比赛，则裁判员应给出清楚的信号使比赛继续。

如果一球队已经累计犯规达到4次且又出现一次累计犯规，而裁判员决定掌握有利，则第三裁判员应在计时台恰当的位置上示意第5次累计犯规。但如果该队在比赛停止前又出现新的累计犯规，则助理裁判员必须发出声音信号，除非对方球队有明显的进球得分机会。

计时器

如果计时器不能正常工作，助理裁判员应通知裁判员。此时计时员应用人工计时器继续计时。在这种情况下，他们应邀请每队各一名官员，以便于通知他们实际的比赛时间。

如果比赛重新开始后，计时员忘记开启计时器，则裁判员应令没有计时的比赛时间补足。

After restarts, the chronometer is started as follows:

- Kick-off: after the ball is kicked towards the opponents' half of the pitch, in accordance with the procedure
- Goal clearance: after the goalkeeper releases the ball from his hands and the ball leaves the penalty area, in accordance with the procedure
- Corner kick: after the ball is kicked and moves, in accordance with the procedure
- Kick-in: after the ball enters the pitch after being kicked, in accordance with the procedure
- Direct free kick outside the penalty areas: after the ball is kicked, in accordance with the procedure
- Indirect free kick outside the penalty areas to either of the teams or taken by the attacking team from the penalty area line: after the ball is kicked, in accordance with the procedure
- Direct or indirect free kick inside the penalty areas to the defending team: after the ball is kicked and leaves the penalty area, in accordance with the procedure
- Penalty kick: after the ball is kicked forward, in accordance with the procedure
- Direct free kick after the fifth accumulated foul: after the ball is kicked with the intention of scoring a goal, in accordance with the procedure
- Dropped ball: after the ball is released from the hands of one of the referees and touches the pitch, in accordance with the procedure

比赛重新开始后，应按照如下情况启动计时器：

- 开球：根据程序，当球被踢向对方半场。
- 球门球：根据程序，当球从守门员的手中掷出且离开罚球区后。
- 角球：根据程序，当球被踢并移动后。
- 踢界外球：根据程序，当球被踢并进入场地后。
- 罚球区外的直接任意球：根据程序，当球被踢后。
- 任一球队罚球区外或攻方在罚球区线上的间接任意球：根据程序，当球被踢后。
- 守方在罚球区内的直接或间接任意球：根据程序，当球被踢并离开罚球区后。
- 罚球点球：根据程序，当球被踢并向前移动后。
- 第5次累计犯规后的直接任意球：根据程序，当球以射门得分为目的被踢出后。
- 坠球：根据程序，当球从其中一名裁判员手中抛出并触及场地。

Time-out

Fifth accumulated foul

暂停

第5次累计犯规

Half-time interval

The referees allow an interval between the two halves if a player of one of the teams requests one, even if the captains of both teams have asked not to have an interval.

Extra time

If extra time is played, there is no interval between the two periods. The teams simply change halves of the pitch and the substitutes and team officials change technical areas.

半场休息

即便双方队长已经要求中场不休息，但如果两队中任一队员提出休息要求，裁判员也应允许中场休息。

加时赛

如果比赛有加时赛，则上下半场之间没有休息。两队仅需交换场地，而替补队员和球队官员则交换技术区域。

Kick-off

- The referees do not have to request the confirmation of the goalkeepers or any other player before ordering the kick-off to be taken

Dropped ball

- Any player may challenge for the ball (including the goalkeeper)
- There is no minimum or maximum number of players for contesting a dropped ball
- The referees cannot decide who may or may not contest a dropped ball
- There is no required distance to be respected by the players, unless the opponent is blocked and the dropped ball cannot be taken
- It is not necessary for a team to contest a dropped ball
- If an infringement is committed by a player before the ball is in play but after one of the referees has released it from his hands, the referee retakes the dropped ball after taking the corresponding disciplinary action

开球

- 开球前，裁判员无需得到守门员或任何其他球员确认。

坠球

- 任何队员都可以参与坠球（包括守门员）。
- 没有参与坠球的最少和最多队员人数。
- 裁判员无权决定某队员是否可以参与坠球。
- 对队员来说，在坠球时没有需要退出的距离，除非阻挡对方，而坠球无法进行。
- 球队不是必须要参与坠球。
- 坠球时在球进入比赛前一队员违规，但其中一名裁判员已经将球从手中抛出，则裁判员应在采取相应的纪律制裁后重新坠球。

The ball inside the pitch touches one of the referees

If, when the ball is in play, it touches one of the referees who is temporarily on the pitch, play continues because the referees are part of the match.

If, when the ball is in play, it touches one of the assistant referees who is temporarily on the pitch, the referees stop play and restart it with a dropped ball from the position of the ball when play was stopped, unless play was stopped inside the penalty area, in which case one of the referees drops the ball on the penalty area line at the point nearest to where the ball was located when play was stopped.

球在场内触及其中一名裁判员

如果比赛中球触碰到临时在场地内的裁判员，比赛应继续，因为裁判员本身是比赛的一部分。

如果比赛中球触碰到临时在场内的助理裁判员，裁判员应停止比赛并在比赛停止时球所在地点以坠球方式重新开始比赛。除非比赛停止时球在罚球区内，在此情况下则应由其中一名裁判员在比赛停止时距球所处地点最近的罚球区线上坠球重新开始比赛。

Goal scored while a person not participating in the match is on the pitch

If, after a goal is scored, the referees realise, before play restarts, that another person was on the pitch at the time that the goal was scored:

- they must disallow the goal if:
  - the other person was an outside agent or official from one of the teams and interfered with play
  - the other person was a player, substitute, sent-off player or official of the team that scored the goal
- they must allow the goal if:
  - the other person was an outside agent and did not interfere with play
  - the other person was a player, substitute, sent-off player or official of the team that conceded the goal

No goal

If one of the referees signals a goal before the ball has passed wholly over the goal line and immediately realises his error, play is restarted with a dropped ball on the penalty area line at the point nearest to where the ball was located when play was stopped.

进球的同时场地上有非比赛人员

如果进球后，在比赛重新开始前，裁判员意识到在进球的同时另有一人在场地上：

- 裁判员必须判进球无效，如果：

– 另外一人是场外因素或其中一球队的官员且干扰了比赛。

– 另外一人是进球一方的球员、替补队员、被罚令出场的队员或该队官员。

- 裁判员必须判进球有效，如果：

– 另外一人是场外因素且未干扰比赛。

– 另外一人是被进球一方的球员、替补队员、被罚令出场的队员或球队官员。

进球无效

如果其中一名裁判员在球未完全越过球门线前示意进球，但随即意识到错误，则应在比赛停止时距球所处地点最近的罚球区线上以坠球重新开始比赛。

There is no offside in futsal.

室内五人制足球没有越位。

Basic requirements for a foul

The following conditions must be met for an offence to be considered a foul:

- It must be committed by a player or substitute who has not correctly followed the substitution procedure
- It must occur on the pitch
- It must occur while the ball is in play

If the referees stop play due to an offence committed outside the pitch (while the ball is in play) and it has not been committed by a player who left the pitch without the referees' permission in order to do so, play must be restarted with a dropped ball from the position of the ball when play was stopped, unless play was stopped inside the penalty area, in which case one of the referees must drop the ball on the penalty area line at the point nearest to where the ball was located when play was stopped.

It is not a foul when two or more players challenge for the ball at the same time with an opponent, if the challenge is legal.

犯规的基本要素

犯规行为应满足下列条件：

- 必须是由队员或没有正确遵守替补程序的替补队员所为。
- 必须发生在比赛场上。
- 必须是在比赛进行中。

如果裁判员由于比赛场地外的犯规而停止比赛（当时在比赛进行中），且犯规不是由未经裁判员允许离开比赛场地的队员造成，则应在比赛停止时球所在地点以坠球重新开始比赛，除非裁判员将比赛停止时球在罚球区内，遇到这种情况，其中的一名裁判员应在比赛停止时距球最近的罚球区线上以坠球重新开始比赛。

如果两名或更多队员同时与一名对方队员争抢球，而此争抢是合法的，则不犯规。

Careless, reckless, using excessive force

"Careless" means that the player has shown a lack of attention or consideration when making a challenge or that he acted without precaution:

- No further disciplinary sanction is needed if a foul is judged to be careless

"Reckless" means that the player has acted with complete disregard for the danger to, or consequences for, his opponent:

- A player who plays in a reckless manner must be cautioned

"Using excessive force" means that the player has far exceeded the necessary use of force and is in danger of injuring his opponent:

- A player who uses excessive force must be sent off

草率地、鲁莽地或使用过分力量

“草率地”表示队员在争抢球时未集中注意力或欠缺考虑，或行为缺少预防措施：

- 如果认定为“草率地”行为，不必给予纪律处罚。

“鲁莽地”表示队员的行为完全不顾及对方的危险，或因他的行为所带来的危险性后果：

- 如果队员以这种态度对待比赛应该被警告。

“使用过分力量”表示队员使用远超出所需的力量，并且使对方有受伤的危险：

- 队员如有“使用过分力量”的行为应被罚令出场。

Charging an opponent

The act of charging is a challenge for space using physical contact within playing distance of the ball without using arms or elbows.

It is an offence to charge an opponent:

- in a careless manner
- in a reckless manner
- using excessive force

Holding an opponent

Holding an opponent includes the act of preventing him from moving past or around using the hands, the arms or the body.

Referees must make an early intervention and deal firmly with holding offences, especially inside the penalty area and when corner kicks, kick-ins or free kicks are being taken.

To deal with these situations, the referees must:

- warn any player holding an opponent before the ball is in play
- caution the player if the holding continues before the ball is in play
- award a direct free kick or penalty kick and caution the player if it happens once the ball is in play

If a defender starts holding an attacker outside the penalty area and continues holding him inside the penalty area, the referees must award a penalty kick.

冲撞对方

冲撞是指在争抢球的范围内用身体而非手臂或肘部争取位置的行为。

下列冲撞对方是犯规：

- 用草率的方式。
- 用鲁莽的方式。
- 使用过分的力量。

阻止对方移动

阻止对方移动是指用手、臂或身体阻止对方移动或转身的行为。

裁判员要及早预防和严格处理阻止对方移动的犯规，特别是在罚球区内和踢角球、踢界外球、罚任意球时。

对待这种情况，裁判员必须：

- 在比赛重新开始前提醒任何阻止对方移动的队员。
- 在比赛重新开始前，如果队员继续有阻止对方移动的行为，要给予警告。
- 一旦比赛重新开始后再次发生应警告犯规队员，并判罚直接任意球或球点球。

如果一名守方队员从罚球区外开始阻止对方移动直到罚球区内仍有此行为，裁判员应判罚球点球。

Disciplinary sanctions

- A caution for unsporting behaviour must be issued when a player holds an opponent to prevent him gaining possession of the ball or taking up an advantageous position
- A player must be sent off if he denies an obvious goalscoring opportunity by holding an opponent
- No further disciplinary action must be taken in other situations of holding an opponent

Restart of play

- Direct free kick from the position where the offence occurred (see Law 13 – Position of free kick) or a penalty kick if the offence occurred inside the penalty area

Handling the ball

Handling the ball involves a deliberate act of a player making contact with the ball with his hand or arm. The referees must take the following into consideration:

- Movement of the hand towards the ball (not the ball towards the hand)
- The distance between the opponent and the ball (unexpected ball)
- The position of the hand does not necessarily mean that there is an infringement (holding it away from the body does not imply intent)
- Touching the ball with an object held in the hand (clothing, shinguard, etc.) counts as deliberately handling the ball
- Hitting the ball with a thrown object (a boot, shinguard, etc.) counts as deliberately handling the ball

纪律处罚

- 当一名队员为阻止对方控制球或抢占有利位置而实施的阻止对方移动的犯规，裁判员应警告队员这种不正当行为。
- 如果一名队员阻止对方移动犯规而破坏了一个明显的进球得分机会，裁判员应将该队员罚令出场。
- 对于其他形式的阻止对方移动的犯规，不需要给予纪律处罚。

比赛重新开始

- 在犯规发生地点踢直接任意球（参见第十三章—任意球的位置），而当犯规发生在罚球区内则踢球点球。

手球

手球意味着队员具有故意用手或臂部触球的行为。裁判员应考虑下列因素：

- 手向球的方向移动（不是球向手移动）。
- 对方和球之间的距离（意外的球）。
- 手的位置不意味着构成犯规（手离开身体不能说明其意图）。
- 用手中的物品（衣服、护腿板等）触球被认定是故意手球。
- 用手掷出的物品（足球鞋、护腿板等）触球被认定是故意手球。

Disciplinary sanctions

There are circumstances when a caution for unsporting behaviour is required when a player deliberately handles the ball, e.g. when a player:

- deliberately handles the ball to prevent an opponent gaining possession
- attempts to score a goal by deliberately handling the ball
- pretends to be playing the ball with one part of his body when he is really doing so with his hand in order to deceive the referees
- tries to prevent a goal or deny a goalscoring opportunity with his hand when the goalkeeper is not inside his penalty area, and fails in his attempt

A player is sent off, however, if he prevents a goal or an obvious goalscoring opportunity by deliberately handling the ball. This punishment arises not from the act of the player deliberately handling the ball but from the unacceptable and unfair intervention that prevented a goal from being scored.

Restart of play

- Direct free kick from the position where the offence occurred (see Law 13 – Position of free kick) or penalty kick

Outside his own penalty area, the goalkeeper has the same restrictions on handling the ball as does any other player. Inside his own penalty area, the goalkeeper cannot be guilty of a handling offence incurring a direct free kick. He can, however, be guilty of several offences that incur an indirect free kick.

纪律处罚

当队员故意手球时，某些情况下属于非体育行为，应给予警告。例如，当一名队员：

- 故意手球阻止对方得球。
- 企图用故意手球得分。
- 假装用身体的某一部位而实际却用手触球以欺骗裁判员。
- 当守门员不在罚球区内时，用手破坏进球或一个进球机会未遂。

无论如何，如果队员用故意手球来阻止进球或一个明显的进球得分机会，队员将被罚令出场。这个判罚不是针对队员故意手球的行为，而是因为这种行为是不可接受的、不公正的阻止了一个进球。

比赛重新开始

- 在犯规发生地点踢直接任意球（参见规则第十三章–任意球的位置）或罚球点球。

在罚球区外，守门员在手球的限制上同其他队员一样对待。在罚球区内，守门员不可能因手球犯规导致被判罚直接任意球。不过，守门员会因违反一些规定而被判罚间接任意球。

Offences committed by goalkeepers

A goalkeeper is considered to be in control of the ball:

- while the ball is between his hands or between his hand and any surface (e.g. ground, own body)
- while holding the ball in his outstretched open hand
- while in the act of bouncing it on the ground or tossing it into the air

When a goalkeeper has gained possession of the ball with his hands, he cannot be challenged by an opponent.

Possession of the ball means that the goalkeeper has control of the ball.

A goalkeeper is not permitted to touch the ball inside his own half of the pitch in the following circumstances:

- If he is in possession of the ball in his own half of the pitch for more than four seconds, whether
  - with his hands inside his penalty area
  - with his feet in his own half of the pitch
  - with his hands inside his penalty area and with his feet in his own half of the pitch

守门员犯规

下列情况视为守门员已经控制球：

- 球在他的两手之间，或在手和任何其他物体表面之间（如地面、自己身体）。
- 伸出胳膊用张开的手控制球时。
- 在向地面拍球或向空中抛球时。

当守门员用手获得球权时，对方队员不得与其争抢。

获得球权意为守门员已经对球取得控制。

下列情况不允许守门员在本方半场内触球：

- 如果他在本方半场内控制球时间超过4秒，无论：
  - 在本方罚球区内用手。
  - 在本方半场内用脚。
  - 在本方罚球区内用手和在本方半场内用脚。

In all these cases, the referee nearest to the goalkeeper must publicly make the four-second count

- If, after playing the ball, he touches it again in his own half of the pitch after it has been deliberately played to him by a team-mate without an opponent playing or touching it
  - the goalkeeper is considered to be in control of the ball by touching it with any part of his body, except if the ball accidentally rebounds off him
- If he touches the ball with his hands inside his own penalty area after it has been kicked to him by a team-mate
- If he touches the ball with his hands inside his own penalty area after he has received it directly from a kick-in by a team-mate

Restart of play

- Indirect free kick from the position where the offence occurred (see Law 13 – Position of free kick)

在上述情况下，距守门员最近的裁判员应公开示意4秒计时。

- 如果守门员传出球后，在未经对方队员触及的情况下，在本方半场内触及同队队员故意传给他的球：
  - 守门员用身体的任何部位触球将被视为控制球，除非球意外地从他身上弹出。
- 如果他在本方罚球区内用手触及同队队员踢给他的球。
- 如果他在本方罚球区内用手触及同队队员直接踢出的界外球。

比赛重新开始

- 在犯规发生地点踢间接任意球（参见规则第十三章—任意球的位置）。

Offences committed against goalkeepers

- It is an offence to prevent a goalkeeper from releasing the ball from his hands, e.g. when he bounces the ball
- Playing the ball or attempting to do so when the goalkeeper is holding it in the palm of his hand
- A player must be penalised for playing in a dangerous manner if he kicks or attempts to kick the ball when the goalkeeper is in the process of releasing it
- It is an offence to restrict the movement of the goalkeeper by unfairly impeding him, e.g. at the taking of a corner kick
- An attacker coming into physical contact with a goalkeeper inside the latter's own penalty area does not imply that any infringement has been committed, except if the attacker jumps at, charges or pushes the goalkeeper in a careless or reckless manner or using excessive force

Restart of play

- If play was stopped because of an offence committed against the goalkeeper as specified in the above paragraph and the referees cannot apply the advantage rule, thereby stopping play, play will be restarted with an indirect free kick from the position where the offence occurred (see Law 13 – Position of free kick), except if the attacker jumped at, charged or pushed the goalkeeper in a careless or reckless manner or using excessive force, in which case the referees, irrespective of the disciplinary action that they take, must restart play with a direct free kick from the position where the offence occurred (see Law 13 – Position of free kick)

对守门员的犯规

- 队员阻止守门员从手中掷球是一种犯规，如当守门员拍球时。
- 争抢或企图争抢守门员手中的球。
- 当守门员从手中掷球时，如果队员踢或企图踢球，裁判员应判罚该队员以危险方式比赛。
- 用不正当的行为阻挡守门员移动是一种犯规，如在踢角球时。
- 进攻队员与在对方罚球区内的守门员发生身体接触并不意味着出现犯规，除非进攻队员草率地、鲁莽地或使用过分力量跳向、冲撞或推守门员。

比赛重新开始

- 如果出现上述情况，裁判员不能掌握有利而停止比赛，应在犯规地点踢间接任意球重新开始比赛（参见规则第十三章－任意球的位置），除非进攻队员草率地、鲁莽地或使用过分力量跳向、冲撞或推守门员。在这种情况下，裁判员在不考虑纪律处罚的情况下，应在犯规地点以直接任意球重新开始比赛（参见规则第十三章－任意球的位置）。

Playing in a dangerous manner

Playing in a dangerous manner is defined as any action that, while trying to play the ball, threatens injury to an opposing player or himself. It is committed with an opponent nearby and prevents the opponent from playing the ball for fear of injuring himself or the other player.

A scissors or bicycle kick is permissible provided that, in the opinion of the referees, it is not dangerous to an opponent.

Playing in a dangerous manner does not necessary involve physical contact between the players. If there is physical contact, the action becomes an offence punishable with a direct free kick or penalty kick. In the case of physical contact, the referees should carefully consider the likelihood that at the very least misconduct has also been committed.

Disciplinary sanctions

- If a player plays in a dangerous manner in a "normal" challenge, the referees should not take any disciplinary action. If the action is made with obvious risk of injury, the referees should caution the player for making a reckless challenge on an opponent
- If a player denies an obvious goalscoring opportunity by playing in a dangerous manner, the referees should send off the player

以危险方式比赛

以危险方式比赛是指，在试图争抢球时任何危及对方或自己的行为。它导致附近的对方队员由于害怕对自己或他人构成伤害而不能争抢球。

如果裁判员认为队员的动作对其他队员不具有危险性，采用剪刀腿或倒钩踢球是允许的。

以危险方式比赛意味着队员之间没有身体接触。如果有身体接触，则构成可判为直接任意球或球点球的犯规。此时，裁判员要认真考虑这种方式在很大程度上存在着不正当行为的发生。

纪律处罚

- 如果队员以危险方式“正常地”参与比赛，裁判员不必采取纪律处罚。如果队员的行为表现出明显的伤害危险，裁判员应以鲁莽地与对方争抢警告犯规队员。

- 如果队员用以危险方式比赛破坏了一个明显的进球得分机会，裁判员应将该队员罚令出场。

Restart of play

- Indirect free kick from the position where the offence occurred (see Law 13 – Position of free kick)
- If there is contact, a different offence has been committed, punishable by a direct free kick or penalty kick, or if the referees consider that the challenge was made in a careless or reckless manner or using excessive force, a different offence has been committed, punishable by a direct free kick or a penalty kick

Impeding the progress of an opponent

Impeding the progress of an opponent means moving into the path of the opponent to obstruct, block, slow down or force a change of direction by an opponent when the ball is not within playing distance of either player.

All players have a right to their position on the pitch, being in the way of an opponent is not the same as moving into the way of an opponent.

Shielding the ball is permitted. A player who places himself between an opponent and the ball for tactical reasons has not committed an offence as long as the ball is kept within playing distance and the player does not hold off the opponent with his arms or body.

比赛重新开始

- 在犯规发生地点踢间接任意球（参见规则第十三章—任意球的位置）。
- 如果有身体接触，则发生了可判为直接任意球或球点球的犯规，或如果裁判员认为该身体接触是草率地、鲁莽地或使用过分力量，则发生另一可判为直接任意球或球点球的犯规。

阻挡对方行进路线

阻挡对方行进路线是指，当球并不在双方队员的争抢距离之内，某队员抢占到对方合理路线去妨碍、阻挡，使对方减慢速度或改变方向。

所有队员在场内都有选择自己位置的权利，本身处在对方路线与抢占对方路线是不一样的。

掩护球是允许的，只要将球控制在合理范围内，并且没有用手臂或身体限制对方行动。队员根据战术需要将自己置于球和对方队员之间并不犯规。

Delaying the restart of play to issue a card

Once the referees have decided to issue a card, whether to caution or send off a player or a substitute, play must not be restarted until the sanction has been administered.

Cautions for unsporting behaviour

There are different circumstances when a player must be cautioned for unsporting behaviour, e.g. if a player:

- commits in a reckless manner one of the seven offences that incur a direct free kick
- commits a foul for the tactical purpose of interfering with or breaking up a promising attack
- holds an opponent for the tactical purpose of pulling the opponent away from the ball or preventing the opponent from getting to the ball
- handles the ball to prevent an opponent gaining possession or developing an attack (other than the goalkeeper inside his own penalty area)
- handles the ball in an attempt to score a goal (irrespective of whether or not the attempt is successful)
- handles the ball while pretending to play it with another part of his body in an attempt to deceive the referees
- tries to prevent a goal or deny a goalscoring opportunity with his hand, not being the goalkeeper inside his penalty area, and fails in his attempt
- attempts to deceive the referees by feigning injury or pretending to have been fouled (simulation)
- changes places with the goalkeeper during play without the referees' permission

对延误比赛重新开始出牌

只要裁判员决定出牌，不管是警告还是罚令出场、是场上队员还是替补队员，必须等到处罚结束后才能重新开始比赛。

对非体育行为给予警告

当一名队员因不正当行为被警告时有多种不同的情况，例如，如果一名队员：

- 以鲁莽的方式犯有可被判罚直接任意球的七种犯规之一。
- 为达到战术目的用犯规干扰或破坏对方的有利进攻。
- 为达到战术目的而阻止对方移动，将对方队员从球旁拽到一边或者阻止对方队员获得球。
- 用手球阻止对方队员得球或组织进攻（守门员在本方罚球区内除外）。
- 企图用手球得分（无论是否得分）。
- 假装用身体另外一部分触球而实际用手触球以企图欺骗裁判员。
- 非守门员在本方罚球区内的情况下，试图用手破坏进球或明显的进球得分机会未遂。
- 企图通过诈伤或假装被犯规以欺骗裁判员（佯装）。
- 比赛中未经裁判员允许和守门员互换位置。

- acts in a manner which shows a lack of respect for the game
- plays the ball when he is walking off the pitch after being granted permission to leave the pitch
- verbally distracts an opponent during play or at a restart
- makes unauthorised marks on the pitch
- uses a deliberate trick while the ball is in play to pass the ball to his own goalkeeper with his head, chest, knee, etc. in order to circumvent Law 12, irrespective of whether the goalkeeper touches the ball with his hands or not. The offence is committed by the player in attempting to circumvent both the letter and the spirit of Law 12 and play is restarted with an indirect free kick

Celebration of a goal

While it is permissible for a player to demonstrate his joy when a goal has been scored, the celebration must not be excessive.

Reasonable celebrations are allowed, but the practice of choreographed celebrations is not to be encouraged when it results in excessive time-wasting and referees are instructed to intervene in such cases.

A player must be cautioned if:

- in the opinion of the referees, he makes gestures which are provocative, derisory or inflammatory
- he climbs on to a perimeter fence to celebrate a goal being scored
- he removes his shirt or covers his head with his shirt, even if he has the same one on underneath
- he covers his head or face with a mask or other similar item

- 表现出一种对比赛不尊重的行为。
- 在获准离开比赛场地而走出场地的过程中触球。
- 比赛中或比赛重新开始时用言语干扰对方。
- 在比赛场地上做未经许可的标记。
- 比赛中队员故意使用诡计，用头、胸或膝盖等部位传球给守门员以回避规则的相关处罚条款，无论守门员是否用手触球，该队员行为是企图规避第十二章的条文和精神内涵而造成的犯规。裁判员应以间接任意球重新开始比赛。

庆祝进球

进球后队员表现出欢庆的行为是允许的，但此行为不能过分。

合理的欢庆是允许的，但自编的表演动作浪费过多时间不应鼓励，裁判员对类似情况应予以干涉。

队员如有下列表现必须被警告：

- 裁判员认为该队员做出的动作具有挑拨性、嘲笑性和煽动性。
- 进球后爬上球场附近的围栏庆祝。
- 脱去上衣或用上衣将头遮住，即使其穿着同样颜色的内衣。
- 用面具或类似物品遮住头部或面部。

Leaving the pitch to celebrate a goal is permitted, but it is essential that players return to the pitch as soon as possible.

Showing dissent by word or action

A player or substitute who is guilty of dissent by protesting (verbally or non-verbally) against the decisions of the referees or assistant referees must be cautioned.

The captain of a team has no special status or privileges under the Futsal Laws of the Game but he has a degree of responsibility for the behaviour of his team.

Any player or substitute who attacks a match official or is guilty of using offensive, rude or obscene gestures or language must be sent off.

Delaying the restart of play

Referees must caution players who delay the restart of play by tactics such as:

- taking a free kick from the wrong position with the sole intention of forcing the referees to order a retake
- kicking the ball away or carrying it away with the hands after the referees have stopped play
- delaying their departure from the pitch after the medical staff come on to assess an injury they have suffered
- provoking a confrontation by deliberately touching the ball after the referees have stopped play

队员离开场地庆祝进球的举动本身是允许的，但关键是队员要尽快回到场内。

用言语或行动表示不满

队员或替补队员用抗议对裁判员的判罚表示不满或攻击（口头或其他形式）必须予以警告。

在室内五人制足球竞赛规则中，球队队长没有特殊的身份和特权，但他要对本队的行为负一定责任。

任何队员或替补队员攻击比赛官员或对其使用无礼的、粗鲁的或下流的姿势或言语必须被罚令出场。

延误比赛重新开始

裁判员必须对下列以战术目的延误比赛重新开始的行为进行警告：

- 在错误的地点踢任意球，其唯一目的是迫使裁判员判罚重踢任意球。
- 在裁判员停止比赛后，将球踢开或用手将球拿走。
- 在队医察看伤情后，队员拖延离开比赛场地的时间。
- 在裁判员停止比赛后，队员故意触球而引发冲突。

Simulation

Any player that tries to fool the referees by feigning injury or pretending to have suffered an offence will be guilty of simulation and will be punished for unsporting behaviour. If the match is stopped as a result of this infringement, play is restarted with an indirect free kick from the position where the offence was committed (see Law 13 – Position of free kick).

Persistent infringement

Referees should be alert at all times to players who persistently infringe the Futsal Laws of the Game. In particular, they must be aware that, even if a player commits a number of different offences, he must still be cautioned for persistently infringing the Futsal Laws of the Game.

There is no specific number of infringements which constitutes "persistence" or the presence of a pattern – this is entirely a matter of judgement and must be determined in the context of effective game management.

佯装

任何队员试图通过诈伤或假装被犯规欺骗裁判员，将视为佯装犯规并被判非体育行为。如果比赛因此而停止，应在犯规地点以间接任意球重新开始比赛（参见规则第十三章—任意球的位置）

持续犯规

裁判员自始至终都应注意那些持续违反室内五人制足球竞赛规则的队员，特别是当裁判员意识到一队员多次犯规，即使其犯规形式不同，但他还是要因持续违反室内五人制足球竞赛规则而受到警告。

对“持续犯规”次数或其表现形式，规则中并没有明确规定，这完全是一个判断问题，而且应根据裁判员对比赛的有效管理而定。

Serious foul play

A player is guilty of serious foul play if he uses excessive force or brutality against an opponent when challenging for the ball when it is in play.

A tackle that endangers the safety of an opponent must be sanctioned as serious foul play.

Any player who lunges at an opponent in challenging for the ball from the front, from the side or from behind using one or both legs, with excessive force and endangering the safety of an opponent is guilty of serious foul play.

Advantage should not be applied in situations involving serious foul play unless there is a clear subsequent opportunity to score a goal. The referees send off the player guilty of serious foul play when the ball is next out of play.

A player who is guilty of serious foul play should be sent off and play is restarted with a direct free kick from the position where the offence occurred (see Law 13 – Position of free kick) or a penalty kick (if the offence occurred inside the offender's penalty area).

严重犯规

比赛中，如果队员故意使用过分的力量或使用野蛮的方式与对方队员争抢球，应被视为严重犯规。

危及对方队员安全的抢截动作，应视为严重犯规。

任何队员用单腿或双腿从对方队员正面、侧面或后面，使用过分的力量且危及对方安全的方式争抢球，均为严重犯规。

当严重犯规发生时裁判员不应运用有利条款，除非有非常明显的进球机会，裁判员应在比赛下一次停止时将严重犯规的队员罚令出场。

队员有严重犯规行为应被罚令出场，裁判员应判直接任意球并在犯规地点重新开始比赛（参见规则第十三章—任意球的位置），或判罚球点球重新开始比赛（如果犯规发生在犯规队员本方罚球区内）。

Violent conduct

A player is guilty of violent conduct if excessive force or brutality is used against an opponent without either of them challenging for the ball.

He is also guilty of violent conduct if he uses excessive force or brutality against a team-mate, spectator, the referees or assistant referees or any other person.

Violent conduct may occur either on the pitch or outside its boundaries, whether the ball is in play or not.

Advantage should not be applied in situations involving violent conduct unless there is a clear subsequent opportunity to score a goal. In such a case, the referees must send off the player guilty of violent conduct when the ball is next out of play.

Referees are reminded that violent conduct often leads to mass confrontation between players, therefore they must try to avert this with strict intervention.

A player or substitute who is guilty of violent conduct must be sent off.

暴力行为

如果队员的目的不是为了球，而对对方使用过分的力量或野蛮的方式，则犯有暴力行为。

如果队员使用过分的力量或野蛮的方式对待队友、观众、裁判员、助理裁判员或任何其他人，也是暴力行为。

无论在比赛进行中或停止时，暴力行为在场内或场外均有可能发生。

涉及暴力行为时裁判员不应掌握有利条款，除非有明显的进球得分机会。在这种情况下，裁判员应在下一次比赛停止时将有暴力行为的队员罚令出场。

提请裁判员，暴力行为常常会导致队员间的大规模冲突，因此裁判员必须严格处理以避免类似事件发生。

有暴力行为的队员或替补队员必须被罚令出场。

Restart of play

- If the ball is out of play, play is restarted according to the previous decision
- If the ball is in play and the offence occurred outside the pitch:
  - if the player is outside the pitch after leaving it in a manner authorized by the Futsal Laws of the Game and commits an infringement, play is restarted with a dropped ball from the position of the ball when play was stopped, unless play was stopped inside the penalty area, in which case one of the referees drops the ball on the penalty area line at the point nearest to where the ball was located when play was stopped
  - if the player leaves the pitch to commit the offence, play is restarted with an indirect free kick from the position in which the ball was located when play was stopped (see Law 13 – Position of free kick)
- If the ball is in play and a player commits an offence inside the pitch:
  - against an opponent:

    play is restarted with a direct free kick from the position where the offence occurred (see Law 13 – Position of free kick) or a penalty kick (if inside the offending player's own penalty area)
  - against a team-mate:

    play is restarted with an indirect free kick from the position where the offence occurred (see Law 13 – Position of free kick)

重新开始比赛

- 如果球出界，根据球出界前的判罚重新开始比赛。
- 如果在比赛进行中而犯规发生在场外：
  - 如果队员离场符合室内五人制足球竞赛规则且犯规发生在场外，则应该在比赛停止时球所在地点以坠球重新开始比赛，除非比赛停止时球在罚球区内，在此情况下其中一名裁判员在距比赛停止时球所在地点最近的罚球区线上以坠球重新开始比赛。

  - 如果队员离开场地犯规，应该在比赛停止时球所在地点以间接任意球重新开始比赛（参见规则第十三章—任意球的位置）。

- 如果在比赛进行中犯规发生在场内：
  - 对对方队员犯规：
    在犯规发生地点以直接任意球（参见第十三章—任意球的位置）或罚球点球（如果在犯规队员本方罚球区内）重新开始比赛。
  - 对同队队员犯规：
    在犯规发生地点以间接任意球重新开始比赛（参见规则第十三章—任意球的位置）。

- against a substitute:
  play is restarted with an indirect free kick to the team of the player who committed the violent conduct from the position of the ball when play was stopped (see Law 13 – Position of free kick), as the illegal entry of the substitute was the first offence committed
- against the referees:
  play is restarted with an indirect free kick from the position where the offence occurred (see Law 13 – Position of free kick)
- against another person:
  play is restarted with a dropped ball from the position of the ball when play was stopped, unless play was stopped inside the penalty area, in which case one of the referees drops the ball on the penalty area line at the point nearest to where the ball was located when play was stopped

• If the ball is in play and a substitute or team official commits an offence outside the pitch:
  - against another person:
    play is restarted with a dropped ball from the position of the ball when play was stopped, unless play was stopped inside the penalty area, in which case one of the referees drops the ball on the penalty area line at the point nearest to where the ball was located when play was stopped

- 对替补队员犯规：

  如果替补队员违规进入场地在先，则判犯有暴力行为的队员所在球队在比赛停止时球所在地点以间接任意球重新开始比赛（参见规则第十三章—任意球的位置）。

- 对裁判员犯规：

  在犯规发生地点以间接任意球重新开始比赛（参见规则第十三章—任意球的位置）。

- 对其他人犯规：

  在比赛停止时球所在地点以坠球重新开始比赛，除非比赛停止时球在罚球区内，在此情况下其中一名裁判员应在距比赛停止时球所在地点最近的罚球区线上以坠球重新开始比赛。

• 如果比赛进行中替补队员或球队官员在场外犯规

  - 对其他人犯规：

    在比赛停止时球所在地点以坠球重新开始比赛，除非比赛停止时球在罚球区内，在此情况下其中一名裁判员应在距比赛停止时球所在地点最近的罚球区线上以坠球重新开始比赛。

Offence where an object is thrown

If, while the ball is in play, a player or substitute throws an object or a ball at an opponent or any other person in a reckless manner, the referees stop play if they cannot apply the advantage and caution the player or substitute.

If while the ball is in play, a player or substitute throws an object or a ball at an opponent or any other person with excessive force, the referees stop play if they cannot apply the advantage to allow an obvious goalscoring opportunity to ensue and send off the player or substitute for violent conduct.

Restart of play

- If a player standing inside his own penalty area throws an object or a ball at an opponent standing outside the penalty area, the referees restart play with a direct free kick to the opposing team taken from the position where the object struck or would have struck the opponent (see Law 13 – Position of free kick)
- If a player standing outside his own penalty area throws an object or a ball at an opponent standing inside the penalty area, the referees restart play with a penalty kick to the opposing team
- If a player standing inside the pitch throws an object or a ball at any person standing outside the pitch, the referees restart play with an indirect free kick to the opposing team from the position of the ball when play was stopped (see Law 13 – Position of free kick); the player is considered to have left the pitch without the referees' permission and for a reason not authorised in the Futsal Laws of the Game

用物品掷击犯规

如果在比赛进行中，一队员或替补队员以鲁莽的方式用物品或球掷击对方或其他人，裁判员如果不能掌握有利，则应停止比赛并警告该队员或替补队员。

如果在比赛进行中，一队员或替补队员使用过分的力量用物品或球掷击对方或其他人，裁判员如果不能确保明显进球得分机会而掌握有利，则应停止比赛，将这名犯有暴力行为的队员或替补队员罚令出场。

比赛重新开始

- 如果一名站在本方罚球区内的队员用物品或球掷击站在罚球区外的对方队员，裁判员应判给对方在物品击中或可能击中对方队员的地点踢直接任意球重新开始比赛（参见规则第十三章—任意球的位置）。

- 如果一名站在本方罚球区外的队员用物品或球掷击站在本方罚球区内的对方队员，裁判员应判给对方罚球点球重新开始比赛。

- 如果一名站在场内的队员用物品或球掷击站在场外的任何人，裁判员应判给对方在比赛停止时球所在地点以间接任意球重新开始比赛（参见规则第十三章—任意球的位置）。该队员则被视为未经裁判员允许离开比赛场地，并且也不符合室内五人制足球竞赛规则。

- If a player standing outside the pitch throws an object or a ball at an opponent standing inside the pitch, the referees restart play with a direct free kick to the opposing team from the position where the object struck or would have struck the opponent or with a penalty kick (if inside the offending player's own penalty area)
- If a substitute standing outside the pitch throws an object or a ball at an opponent standing inside the pitch, the referees restart play with an indirect free kick to the opposing team from the position of the ball when play was stopped (see Law 13 – Position of free kick); the substitute is considered to have entered the pitch without the referees' permission and without following the substitution procedure
- If a substitute standing inside the pitch, causing his team to have an extra player, throws an object or a ball at any person standing inside or outside the pitch, the referees restart play with an indirect free kick to the opposing team from the position of the ball when play was stopped (see Law 13 – Position of free kick); the substitute is considered to have entered the pitch without the referees' permission
- If a substitute who has infringed the substitution procedure throws an object or the ball at any person standing inside or outside the pitch, he is treated as if he were a player
- If a team official standing inside or outside the pitch throws an object or a ball at any person standing inside or outside the pitch, the referees restart play with a dropped ball from the position of the ball when play was stopped, unless play was stopped inside the penalty area, in which case one of the referees drops the ball on the penalty area line at the point nearest to where the ball was located when play was stopped

- 如果一名站在场外的队员用物品或球掷击站在场内的对方队员，裁判员应判给对方在物品击中或可能击中对方队员的地点踢直接任意球或罚球点球重新开始比赛（如果在犯规队员的本方罚球区内）。
- 如果一名替补队员站在场外用物品或球掷击场内的对方队员，裁判员应判给对方在比赛停止时球所在的地点踢间接任意球重新开始比赛（参见规则第十三章—任意球的位置）。该替补队员则被视为未经裁判员许可进入比赛场地且没有遵守替补程序。
- 如果一名替补队员站在场地内，造成其队多出一名队员，同时他用物品或球掷击场内任何人，裁判员应判给对方在比赛停止时球所在地点踢间接任意球重新开始比赛（参见规则第十三章—任意球的位置）。该替补队员则被视为未经裁判员许可进入比赛场地。
- 如果一名替补队员已经违反替补程序，之后用物品或球掷击站在场内或场外的任何人，将被视为场上队员进行处理。
- 如果一名球队官员站在场内或场外用物品或球掷击站在场内或场外的任何人，裁判员应在比赛停止时球所在地点以坠球重新开始比赛，除非比赛在罚球区内被停止，在此情况下其中一名裁判员应在比赛停止时距球所在地点最近的罚球区线上以坠球重新开始比赛。

Offences where an object is thrown at the ball

If a player other than one of the goalkeepers throws an object or a ball at the ball:

- if the ball is in play and the object strikes the ball, the referees must stop play and caution him for unsporting behaviour or send him off if by doing so he denied a goal or an obvious goalscoring opportunity. They restart play with a direct free kick to the opposing team from the position of the ball when play was stopped (see Law 13 – Position of free kick) or a penalty kick if the ball was inside the offending team's penalty area
- if the ball is in play and the object does not strike the ball, the referees must stop play if they cannot apply the advantage and caution him for unsporting behaviour. They restart play with an indirect free kick to the opposing team from the position of the ball when play was stopped (see Law 13 – Position of free kick)

If one of the two goalkeepers throws an object or a ball at the ball:

- if the ball is in play and the object strikes the ball inside the goalkeeper's penalty area, the referees must stop play and caution him for unsporting behaviour. They restart play with an indirect free kick to the opposing team from the position of the ball when play was stopped (see Law 13 – Position of free kick)

用物品向球掷击犯规

如果除守门员之外的队员用物品或球掷击球：

- 如果在比赛进行中该物品击中球，裁判员必须停止比赛并因非体育行为警告该队员，或因其破坏进球或一个明显的进球得分机会而将该队员罚令出场。裁判员应判给对方在比赛停止时球所在地点踢直接任意球（参见规则第十三章—任意球的位置），或当球在犯规方罚球区内时以罚球点球重新开始比赛。

- 如果在比赛进行中该物品未击中球，裁判员在不能掌握有利的情况下，应停止比赛并以非体育行为警告该队员。裁判员判给对方在比赛停止时球所在地点踢间接任意球重新开始比赛（参见规则第十三章—任意球的位置）。

如果守门员用物品或球掷击球：

- 如果在比赛进行中该物品在守门员本方罚球区内击中球，裁判员应停止比赛并以非体育行为警告该队员。裁判员应判给对方在比赛停止时球所在地点踢间接任意球重新开始比赛（参见规则第十三章—任意球的位置）。

- if the ball is in play and the object strikes the ball outside the goalkeeper's penalty area, the referees must stop play and caution him for unsporting behaviour or send him off if by doing so he denied a goal or an obvious goalscoring opportunity. They restart play with a direct free kick to the opposing team from the position of the ball when play was stopped
- if the ball is in play and the object does not strike the ball, the referees must stop play if they cannot apply the advantage and caution him for unsporting behaviour. They restart play with an indirect free kick to the opposing team from the position of the ball when play was stopped (see Law 13 – Position of free kick)

If a player, including the two goalkeepers, directs an object at the ball with a part of his body other than his hands:

- if the ball is in play and the object strikes the ball, the referees must stop play and caution him for unsporting behaviour. They restart play with an indirect free kick to the opposing team from the position of the ball when play was stopped (see Law 13 – Position of free kick)
- if the ball is in play and the object does not strike the ball, the referees must stop play if they cannot apply the advantage and caution him for unsporting behaviour. They restart play with an indirect free kick to the opposing team from the position of the ball when play was stopped (see Law 13 – Position of free kick)

If a substitute infringing the substitution procedure but not causing his team to play with an extra player throws an object at the ball:

- 如果在比赛进行中该物品在守门员本方罚球区外击中球，裁判员应停止比赛并以非体育行为警告该队员，或因其破坏进球或一个明显的进球得分机会而将其罚令出场。裁判员应判给对方在比赛停止时球所在地点踢直接任意球重新开始比赛。
- 如果在比赛进行中该物品没有击中球，裁判员在不能掌握有利的情况下，应停止比赛并以非体育行为警告该队员。裁判员应判给对方在比赛停止时球所在地点踢间接任意球重新开始比赛（参见规则第十三章—任意球的位置）。

如果一名队员（包括两名守门员）用身体的一部分而非用手将一物品击向球：

- 如果在比赛进行中该物品击中球，裁判员应停止比赛并因非体育行为警告该队员。裁判员应判给对方在比赛停止时球所在地点踢间接任意球重新开始比赛（参见规则第十三章—任意球的位置）。
- 如果在比赛进行中该物品未击中球，裁判员在不能掌握有利的情况下，应停止比赛并以非体育行为警告该队员。裁判员应判给对方在比赛停止时球所在地点踢间接任意球重新开始比赛（参见规则第十三章—任意球的位置）。

如果一名替补队员违反替补程序，但没有造成其所在球队场上多一人的情况下用物品掷击球：

- if the ball is in play and the object strikes the ball, the referees must stop play and either send him off for a double caution, the first caution for entering the pitch without following the substitution procedure and the second for unsporting behaviour, or send him off directly if by doing so he denied a goal or an obvious goalscoring opportunity. They restart play with a direct free kick to the opposing team from the position of the ball when play was stopped (see Law 13 – Position of free kick) or a penalty kick if the ball was inside the substitute's penalty area
- if the ball is in play and the object does not strike the ball, the referees must stop play if they cannot apply the advantage and send him off for a double caution, the first caution for entering the pitch without following the substitution procedure and the second for unsporting behaviour. They restart play with an indirect free kick to the opposing team from the position of the ball when play was stopped (see Law 13 – Position of free kick)

If a substitute infringing the substitution procedure but not causing his team to be playing with an extra player directs an object at the ball with a part of his body other than his hands:

- if the ball is in play and the object strikes the ball, the referees must stop play and either send him off for a double caution, the first caution for entering the pitch without following the substitution procedure and the second for unsporting behaviour, or send him off directly if by doing so he denied a goal or an obvious goalscoring opportunity. They restart play with an indirect free kick to the opposing team from the position of the ball when play was stopped (see Law 13 – Position of free kick)

- 如果在比赛进行中该物品击中球，裁判员必须停止比赛，要么两次警告该队员从而将其罚令出场，第一次因为该队员没有遵守替补程序进入比赛场地，第二次则因为非体育行为；要么因为其破坏进球或明显的进球得分机会而直接罚令出场。裁判员应判给对方在比赛停止时球所在地点踢直接任意球重新开始比赛（参见规则第十三章—任意球的位置），或由于球在该替补队员所在球队的罚球区内而判罚球点球重新开始比赛。
- 如果在比赛进行中该物品没有击中球，裁判员如果在不能掌握有利的情况下，应停止比赛并两次警告该队员从而将其罚令出场，第一次因为该队员没有遵守替补程序进入比赛场地，第二次则因为非体育行为。裁判员应判给对方在比赛停止时球所在地点踢间接任意球重新开始比赛（参见规则第十三章—任意球的位置）。

如果一名替补队员违反替补程序，但没有造成其所在球队场上多一人的情况下，用身体的一部分而非用手将一物品击向球：

- 如果在比赛进行中该物品击中球，裁判员应停止比赛。要么两次警告该队员从而将其罚令出场，第一次因为该队员没有遵守替补程序进入比赛场地，第二次则因为非体育行为；要么因为其破坏进球或明显的进球得分机会而直接罚令出场。裁判员应判给对方在比赛停止时球所在地点踢间接任意球重新开始比赛（参见规则第十三章—任意球的位置）。

- if the ball is in play and the object does not strike the ball, the referees must stop play if they cannot apply the advantage and send him off for a double caution, the first caution for entering the pitch without following the substitution procedure and the second for unsporting behaviour. They restart play with an indirect free kick to the opposing team from the position of the ball when play was stopped (see Law 13 – Position of free kick)

If a substitute throws an object at the ball, thus causing his team to be playing with an extra player:

- if the ball is in play and the object strikes the ball, the referees must stop play and either send him off for a double caution, both for unsporting behaviour, the first caution for entering the pitch without the referees' permission and the second for throwing the object, or send him off directly if by doing so he denied a goal or an obvious goalscoring opportunity. They restart play with an indirect free kick to the opposing team from the position of the ball when play was stopped (see Law 13 – Position of free kick)
- if the ball is in play and the object does not strike the ball, the referees must stop play if they cannot apply the advantage and send him off for a double caution, both for unsporting behaviour, the first caution for entering the pitch without the referees' permission and the second for throwing the object. They restart play with an indirect free kick to the opposing team from the position of the ball when play was stopped (see Law 13 – Position of free kick)

- 如果在比赛进行中该物品没有击中球，裁判员在不能掌握有利的情况下，应停止比赛并两次警告该队员从而将其罚令出场，第一次因为该队员没有遵守替补程序进入比赛场地，第二次则因为非体育行为。裁判员应判给对方在比赛停止时球所在地点踢间接任意球重新开始比赛（参见规则第十三章—任意球的位置）。

如果一名替补队员向球掷击一物品，并因此造成其所在球队场上多一人：

- 如果在比赛进行中该物品击中球，裁判员应停止比赛。要么两次因非体育行为警告该队员从而将其罚令出场，第一次警告因为该队员未经裁判员许可进入比赛场地，第二次则因为其投掷物品；要么因为其破坏进球或明显的进球得分机会而直接罚令出场。裁判员应判给对方在比赛停止时球所在地点踢间接任意球重新开始比赛（参见规则第十三章—任意球的位置）。

- 如果在比赛进行中该物品没有击中球，裁判员如果在不能掌握有利的情况下，应停止比赛并两次因非体育行为警告该队员从而将其罚令出场，第一次警告因为该队员未经裁判员许可进入比赛场地，第二次则因为其投掷物品。裁判员应判给对方在比赛停止时球所在地点踢间接任意球重新开始比赛（参见规则第十三章—任意球的位置）。

If a substitute directs an object at the ball with a part of his body other than his hands, thus causing his team to be playing with an extra player:

- if the ball is in play and the object strikes the ball, the referees must stop play and either send him off for a double caution, both for unsporting behaviour, the first caution for entering the pitch without the referees' permission and the second for directing the object, or send him off directly if by doing so he denied a goal or an obvious goalscoring opportunity. They restart play with an indirect free kick to the opposing team from the position of the ball when play was stopped (see Law 13 – Position of free kick)
- if the ball is in play and the object does not strike the ball, the referees must stop play if they cannot apply the advantage and send him off for a double caution, both for unsporting behaviour, the first caution for entering the pitch without the referees' permission and the second for throwing the object. They restart play with an indirect free kick to the opposing team from the position of the ball when play was stopped (see Law 13 – Position of free kick)

If a team official directs an object at the ball with any part of his body:

- if the ball is in play and the object strikes the ball, the referees must stop play and expel him from the technical area and its surrounds. Play is restarted with a dropped ball from the position of the ball when play was stopped, unless play was stopped inside the penalty area, in which case one of the referees drops the ball on the penalty area line at the point nearest to where the ball was located when play was stopped

如果一名替补队员用身体的一部分而非用手将一物品击向球，并因此造成其所在球队场上多一人：

- 如果在比赛进行中该物品击中球，裁判员必须停止比赛。要么两次因非体育行为警告该队员从而将其罚令出场，第一次警告因为该队员未经裁判员许可进入比赛场地，而第二次则因为其投掷物品；要么因为其破坏进球或明显的进球得分机会而直接罚令出场。裁判员应判给对方在比赛停止时球所在地点踢间接任意球重新开始比赛（参见规则第十三章—任意球的位置）。
- 如果在比赛进行中该物品没有击中球，裁判员在不能掌握有利的情况下，应停止比赛并两次因非体育行为警告该队员从而将其罚令出场，第一次警告因为该队员未经裁判员许可进入比赛场地，第二次则因为其投掷物品。裁判员应判给对方在比赛停止时球所在地点踢间接任意球重新开始比赛（参见规则第十三章—任意球的位置）。

如果一名球队官员使用身体的任何一部分用物品掷击球：

- 如果在比赛进行中该物品击中球，裁判员应停止比赛并将其逐出技术区域及附近区域。裁判员应在比赛停止时球所在地点以坠球重新开始比赛，除非比赛停止时球在罚球区内，在此情况下其中一名裁判员应在比赛停止时距球所在地点最近的罚球区线上以坠球重新开始比赛。

- if the ball is in play and the object does not strike the ball, the referees must stop play if they cannot apply the advantage and expel him from the technical area and its surrounds. Play is restarted with a dropped ball from the position of the ball when play was stopped, unless play was stopped inside the penalty area, in which case one of the referees drops the ball on the penalty area line at the point nearest to where the ball was located when play was stopped

If the ball is not in play and a player throws an object at the ball, the referees caution him for unsporting behaviour. Play is restarted in accordance with the Futsal Laws of the Game.

If the ball is not in play and a substitute throws an object at the ball, whether he causes his team to be playing with an extra player or not, the referees send him off for a double caution, both for unsporting behaviour, the first caution for entering the pitch without the referees' permission and the second for throwing the object.

If the ball is not in play and a team official throws an object at the ball, the referees expel him from the technical area and its surrounds.

Denying a goal or a goalscoring opportunity

There are two sending-off offences that deal with denying an opponent an obvious opportunity to score a goal. It is not necessary for the offence to occur inside the penalty area.

- 如果在比赛进行中该物品没有击中球，裁判员在不能掌握有利的情况下，应停止比赛并将其逐出技术区域及附近区域。裁判员应在比赛停止时球所在地点以坠球重新开始比赛，除非比赛停止时球在罚球区内，在此情况下其中一名裁判员应在比赛停止时距球所在地点最近的罚球区线上以坠球重新开始比赛。

如果比赛停止而一队员用物品掷击球，则裁判员因非体育行为警告该队员。依照室内五人制足球竞赛规则重新开始比赛。

如果比赛停止而一替补队员用物品掷击球，无论是否造成其所在球队场上多一人，裁判员则两次因非体育行为警告该队员从而将其罚令出场，第一次警告该队员未经裁判员许可进入比赛场地，而第二次则因其投掷物品。

如果比赛停止而一球队官员用物品掷击球，裁判员则将其逐出技术区域及附近区域。

阻止进球或一个明显进球得分机会

有两种罚令出场的犯规涉及破坏对方明显的进球机会。这种犯规不必非发生在罚球区内。

If the referees apply the advantage during an obvious goalscoring opportunity and a goal is scored directly, despite the opponent handling the ball deliberately, the player cannot be sent off but he may still be cautioned.

If the referees apply the advantage during an obvious goalscoring opportunity and a goal is scored directly, despite the opponent committing a foul, the player cannot be sent off for the foul itself but he may still be cautioned or sent off if the action in itself warrants a caution or sending-off.

Referees should consider the following circumstances when deciding whether to send off a player for denying a goal or an obvious goalscoring opportunity:

- The distance between the offence and the goal
- The likelihood of keeping or gaining control of the ball
- The direction of the play
- The location and number of defenders
- The offence which denies an opponent an obvious goalscoring opportunity may be an offence that incurs a direct free kick or an indirect free kick
- If the infringement is committed by a substitute, he must always be sent off

If a player attempts to prevent a goal by deliberately handling the ball after a restart of play in which it is not possible to score a goal directly, he is not sent off, but is cautioned for unsporting behaviour. His team is penalised by a direct free kick or a penalty kick.

If a substitute enters the pitch with the aim of denying a goal or a goalscoring opportunity, he is sent off whether or not he achieves his objective.

如果裁判员在出现明显的射门得分机会过程中掌握有利并且进球得分，尽管对方故意手球，但该队员不应被罚令出场，而仍然应被警告。

如果裁判员在出现明显的射门得分机会过程中掌握有利并且进球得分，尽管对方队员犯规，但该队员不应因这一犯规而被罚令出场，然而他仍然可能会因为其动作本身构成可警告或罚令出场的犯规。

裁判员在决定是否将阻止进球或明显进球得分机会的队员罚令出场时应考虑以下情况：

- 犯规地点和守方球门之间的距离。
- 掌握或获得控制球的可能性。
- 可能发展的方向。
- 防守队员的位置和人数。
- 破坏对方明显进球得分机会的犯规应是一种可判直接任意球或间接任意球的犯规。
- 如果此犯规由替补队员造成，他必须被罚令出场。

在直接进球得分无效的方式下重新开始比赛时，如果队员试图故意用手球阻止进球，那么他不应被罚令出场，但是仍将因非体育行为被警告。他所在球队将被判罚直接任意球或球点球。

如果一名替补队员进入场地试图阻止进球或进球得分机会，则无论其是否达到目的，都将被罚令出场。

Procedure

- The ball is in play when it is kicked and moves
- A free kick can be taken by lifting the ball with a foot or both feet simultaneously
- Feinting to take a free kick to confuse opponents is permitted as part of futsal. However, if in the opinion of the referees the feinting is considered an act of unsporting behaviour, the player must be cautioned
- If a player, while correctly taking a free kick, intentionally kicks the ball at an opponent in order to play the ball again but neither in a careless nor a reckless manner nor using excessive force, the referees must allow play to continue
- An indirect free kick must be retaken if the referees fail to raise their arms to indicate that the kick is indirect and the ball is kicked directly into the goal. The initial indirect free kick is not nullified by the referees' mistake
- If, as part of a playing movement, a goalkeeper ends up outside his goal or he or any other player end up outside the pitch, the opposing team may take a direct free kick quickly, provided that they have not committed their sixth accumulated foul
- If the ball bursts after hitting one of the goalposts or the crossbar and does not enter the goal, the referees do not order the free kick to be retaken; they stop play and restart it with a dropped ball from the position of the ball when it burst (see Law 8 – Dropped ball)

程序

- 当球被踢并移动时，比赛开始。
- 任意球可以用单脚或双脚同时将球挑起来踢。
- 在踢任意球时，用假动作迷惑对方作为足球比赛的一部分是允许的。然而，如果裁判员认为队员的假动作属于非体育行为，则该队员应被警告。
- 如果一名队员正确地踢出任意球，但却故意踢向对方，目的是为了可以第二次触球，而且没有采用草率地、鲁莽地或使用过分力量的方式，裁判员应允许比赛继续。
- 当裁判员没有举手示意是间接任意球时，球被直接踢进了球门，应重踢间接任意球。最初的判罚间接任意球不能因裁判员的失误而取消。
- 作为移动的一部分，当比赛停止时守门员处在本方球门之外或任何队员处在场地之外时，如果该队没有达到第6次累计犯规，对方可以快速发出直接任意球。
- 如果球击中其中一个球门柱或横梁后破裂而未进入球门，任意球不应重踢。但裁判员要停止比赛，在球破裂的地点坠球重新开始比赛（参见规则第八章—坠球）。

- If the player taking a direct free kick, beginning with a team's sixth accumulated foul, kicks the ball forward to enable a team-mate to strike at goal, the referees stop play if they cannot apply the advantage and restart it with an indirect free kick from the place where the kicker' s team-mate touched the ball (see Law 13 – Position of free kick)
- If the referees order a free kick to be retaken, the new free kick can be taken by any player and does not have to be taken by the player who did so originally
- If a player takes a direct or indirect free kick before the referees give the signal for it to be taken and before a team's sixth accumulated foul, provided that the team taking the kick has requested their opponents to respect the required distance, the referees stop play if they cannot apply the advantage, order the free kick to be retaken and caution the player
- If a player takes a direct free kick before the referees give the signal for it to be taken, beginning with a team's sixth accumulated foul, they order the free kick to be retaken and caution him
- If a period of play is extended to allow a direct free kick to be taken, beginning with the sixth accumulated foul, and the ball hits one of the goalposts or the crossbar or the goalkeeper before crossing the goal line between the goalposts and the crossbar, the referees award a goal
- If a period of play is extended is allow a direct free kick to be taken, beginning with the sixth accumulated foul, the referees allow the defending goalkeeper to be replaced by an outfield player or an eligible substitute, although in the latter case the substitution procedure must be followed

- 如果队员主罚第6次累计犯规起的直接任意球时，将球向前踢出，以便队友接球射门，裁判员如果不能掌握有利，则应停止比赛并在主罚队员队友触球的地点以间接任意球重新开始比赛（参见规则第十三章—任意球位置）。
- 如果裁判员判重踢任意球，则该任意球可以由任何队员踢出，而不必是原先踢任意球的队员。
- 在罚任意球的球队要求对方退出规定距离的情况下，如果主罚队员在裁判员给予相应的信号之前踢出第6次累计犯规前的直接或间接任意球，裁判员如果不能掌握有利则应停止比赛，判重踢任意球并警告该队员。
- 当主罚队员在裁判员给出信号前踢出第6次累计犯规起的直接任意球，裁判员应判重踢任意球并警告该队员。
- 当半场比赛被延长至允许踢完从第6次累计犯规起的任意球时，如果球在进入球门之前击中其中一个球门柱、横梁或守门员，则裁判员应判进球有效。
- 当半场比赛被延长至允许踢完从第6次累计犯规起的任意球时，裁判员允许守方用场上队员或其他合法替补队员替换守门员，但必须遵守替补程序。

Distance

If a player decides to take a free kick quickly and an opponent who is less than 5m from the ball intercepts it, the referees must allow play to continue.

If a player decides to take a free kick quickly and an opponent who is near the ball deliberately prevents him from taking the kick, the referees must caution the opponent for delaying the restart of play.

If, when a free kick is taken by the defending team from inside its own penalty area, one or more opponents remain inside the penalty area because the defender decided to take the kick quickly and the opponents did not have time to leave the penalty area, the referees must allow play to continue if the ball leaves the penalty area directly without touching another player.

距离

如果队员决定快速踢出任意球，而在距球不足5米的一名防守队员将球拦截，裁判员应允许比赛继续。

如果队员决定快速踢出任意球，而在球附近的一名防守队员故意阻止其踢球，裁判员应警告守方队员延误比赛重新开始。

当守方在本方罚球区内罚任意球时，若守方队员决定快速踢出任意球而此时一名或多名对方队员没有足够时间离开罚球区而仍然滞留在罚球区内，如果球在未触及其他队员的情况下直接离开罚球区，裁判员应允许比赛继续。

Infringements beginning with the sixth accumulated foul – after the whistle and before the ball is in play

	Outcome of the kick	
Infrigements	Goal	No goal
Attacking player	Free kick is retaken	Indirect free kick
Kicker does not shoot at goal	——	Indirect free kick
Kick by unidentified player	Indirect free kick	Indirect free kick
Defending player	Goal	Free kick is retaken
By both teams	Free kick is retaken	Free kick is retaken

第6次累计犯规起的罚球违规 — 在裁判员鸣哨后而比赛重新开始前

	罚球结果	
违规	进球	非进球
进攻队员	重踢任意球	间接任意球
主罚队员未将球射向球门	——	间接任意球
非主罚队员踢球	间接任意球	间接任意球
防守队员	进球	重踢任意球
双方队员	重踢任意球	重踢任意球

Procedure

- Feinting in the run-up to take a penalty kick to confuse opponents is permitted as part of futsal. However, feinting to kick the ball once the player has completed his run-up is considered an infringement of Law 14 and an act of unsporting behaviour for which the player must be cautioned
- If the ball bursts after hitting one of the goalposts or the crossbar and enters the goal, the referees award the goal
- If the ball bursts after hitting one of the goalposts or the crossbar and does not enter the goal, the referees do not order the penalty kick to be retaken but stop play, which is restarted with a dropped ball on the penalty area line at the point nearest to where the ball was located when it burst
- If the player taking the penalty kick kicks the ball forward to enable a teammate to shoot at goal, the referees allow the goal if the procedure for the penalty kick stipulated in Law 14 was observed
- If the referees order the penalty kick to be retaken, the new penalty kick can be taken by any player and does not have to be taken by the player who did so originally
- If the kicker takes the penalty kick before the referees give the signal, they order the penalty kick to be retaken and caution him
- If a period of play is extended to allow a penalty kick to be taken and the ball hits one of the goalposts or the crossbar or the goalkeeper before crossing the goal line between the goalposts and the crossbar, the referees award a goa

程序

- 作为室内五人制足球的一部分，在踢球点球助跑过程中使用假动作迷惑对方是允许的；但在完成助跑后假装踢球将被视为违反规则第十四章的规定，是一种应被警告的非体育行为。
- 如果球射中任何一球门柱或横梁后破裂并进入球门，则裁判员判进球有效。
- 如果球射中任何一球门柱或横梁后破裂未进入球门，裁判员不应判重罚球点球，而要在停止比赛时距球破裂地点最近的罚球区线上坠球重新开始比赛。
- 如果主罚队员将球向前踢出，以便其队友能够接球射门，而罚球点球的整个程序符合规则第十四章规定，裁判员应判进球有效。
- 如果裁判员判重罚球点球，则这个罚球点球可以由任何队员踢出，而不必是原先主罚球点球的队员。
- 如果主罚队员在裁判员鸣哨前踢出球点球，则裁判员应判重罚球点球并警告该队员。
- 如果半场比赛被延长至执行完罚球点球，当球在越过球门柱和横梁之间的球门线之前射中任何一球门柱、横梁或守门员，裁判员应判进球有效。

- If a period of play is extended is allow a penalty kick to be taken, the referees allow the defending goalkeeper to be replaced by an outfield player or an eligible substitute, although in the latter case the substitution procedure must be followed

Preparing for the penalty kick

The referees must confirm the following requirements before the penalty kick is taken:

- The kicker is identified
- The ball is properly placed on the penalty mark
- The goalkeeper is on the goal line between the goalposts and facing the kicker
- The team-mates of the kicker are:
  - outside the penalty area
  - 5m from the ball
  - behind the ball

- 如果半场比赛被延长至执行完罚球点球，裁判员允许守方守门员被其他队员或其他合法替补队员替换，但后一种情况必须遵守替补程序。

罚球点球的准备工作

在罚球点球之前，裁判员必须确认下列必要条件：

- 确认主罚队员。
- 球正确地放在罚球点上。
- 守门员站在两球门柱之间的球门线上，面向主罚队员。
- 主罚队员的队友应在：
  - 罚球区外。
  - 距球5米之外。
  - 在球的后面。

Infringements – after the whistle and before the ball is in play

	Outcome of the kick	
Infrigements	Goal	No goal
Attacking player	Penalty is retaken	Indirect free kick
Kicker kicks backwards	——	Indirect free kick
Kick by unidentified player	Indirect free kick	Indirect free kick
Defending player	Goal	Penalty is retaken
By both teams	Penalty is retaken	Penalty is retaken

If an attacker or defender commits an infringement on an opposing player before the ball is in play, but after one of the referees has given the order to take the kick, they allow the kick to be taken. If a goal is scored and the infringement was committed by the defending team, they award a goal; if the infringement was committed by the attacking team, they order the penalty kick to be retaken. If no goal is scored and the infringement was committed by the defending team, they order the penalty kick to be retaken; if the infringement was committed by the kicker's team, they penalise his team with an indirect free kick from the place where the infringement was committed (see Law 13 – Position of free kick). Furthermore, the referees take the appropriate disciplinary action.

违规 — 在裁判员鸣哨后而比赛重新开始前

	罚球结果	
违规	进球	非进球
进攻队员	重踢球点球	间接任意球
主罚队员向后踢球	间接任意球	间接任意球
非主罚队员踢球	间接任意球	间接任意球
防守队员	进球	重踢球点球
双方队员	重踢球点球	重踢球点球

如果一进攻队员或一防守队员在其中一名裁判员示意踢球点球之后、比赛重新开始前对对方队员犯规，裁判员应允许球点球踢出。如果球进门，而犯规的是防守方，裁判员应判进球有效；如果犯规的是进攻方，裁判员则判重踢球点球。如果球未进门，而犯规的是防守方，裁判员应判重踢球点球；如果犯规的是进攻方，裁判员则应判由对方在犯规地点踢间接任意球重新开始比赛（参见规则第十三章—任意球的位置）。此外，裁判员还应给予相应的纪律制裁。

Procedures for infringements

Referees are reminded that opponents may be no closer than 5m from the point at which the kick-in is to be taken. Where necessary, the referees must warn any player within this distance before the kick-in is taken and caution the player if he subsequently fails to retreat to the correct distance. Play is restarted with a kick-in, and the four-second count begins again if it has already started.

If a player, while correctly taking a kick-in, intentionally kicks the ball at an opponent in order to play the ball again but neither in a careless nor a reckless manner nor using excessive force, the referees must allow play to continue.

If the ball enters the opponents' goal directly from a kick-in, the referees must award a goal clearance. If the ball enters the taker's own goal directly from a kick-in, the referees must award a corner kick.

If the ball does not enter the pitch from a kick-in, the referees shall order a player from the opposing team to take it

If a goalkeeper, as part of a playing movement, ends up outside his goal or he or any other player end up outside the pitch, the opposing team may take the kick-in quickly.

If a kick-in is taken incorrectly, the referees may not apply the advantage even if the ball goes directly to an opponent, but order a player from the opposing team to retake it.

程序违规

提请裁判员注意，在踢界外球时守方队员距踢界外球的位置不应少于5米。如果需要，在踢界外球前裁判员应提醒那些距离过近的守方队员；如果接下来仍然有队员违规，裁判员应给予警告。以踢界外球重新开始比赛，在队员准备好发球后，重新开始4秒计时。

当队员正确踢出界外球但却故意将球踢向对方队员，其目的是为了第二次触球，只要不是以草率地、鲁莽地或使用过分力量的方式，裁判员应允许比赛继续。

如果踢界外球直接进入对方球门，裁判员应判给对方掷球门球。如果踢界外球直接进入本方球门，裁判员应判给对方踢角球。

如果球没有进入比赛场地，裁判员判由对方踢界外球。

作为移动的一部分，当比赛停止时守门员处在本方球门之外或任何队员处在场地之外时，对方可以快速踢出界外球。

如果踢界外球没有被正确踢出，即使是球直接踢给了对方，裁判员也不应掌握有利，而是判由对方队员踢界外球。

Procedures for infringements

If an opponent enters the penalty area or is still in it before the ball is in play and is fouled by a player from the defending team, the goal clearance is retaken and the defender may be cautioned or sent off depending on the nature of the offence.

If, when a goal clearance is taken by the goalkeeper, one or more opponents are still inside the penalty area because the goalkeeper decided to take the clearance quickly and the opponents did not have time to leave the area, the referees must allow play to continue if the ball leaves the penalty area directly without touching another player.

If the goalkeeper, while correctly taking a goal clearance, intentionally throws the ball at an opponent located outside the penalty area but neither in a careless nor a reckless manner nor using excessive force, the referees must allow play to continue.

If, when taking the goal clearance, the goalkeeper does not release the ball from inside his penalty area, the referees order the goal clearance to be retaken, although the four-second count continues from where it was stopped once the goalkeeper is ready to retake it.

It is not necessary for the goalkeeper to have the ball in his hands before the referees begin the four-second count.

程序违规

当对方队员进入罚球区或比赛重新开始前仍在罚球区内时，防守队员对其犯规，球门球应重掷，可根据其犯规性质给予警告或罚令出场。

当守门员掷球门球时，一名或多名对方队员仍处在罚球区内，或因为守门员决定快速掷球门球而没有时间离开罚球区，如果球在未触及其他队员的情况下直接离开罚球区，裁判员应允许比赛继续。

如果守门员在正确掷出球门球时，故意将球掷向罚球区外的对方队员，但并不是以草率地、鲁莽地或使用过分力量的方式，则裁判员应允许比赛继续。

如果在掷球门球时，守门员没能从罚球区内掷出球，裁判员应令其重掷，但4秒计时在守门员准备好再次掷球门球时继续进行。

裁判员4秒计时不必等到守门员手中持球才开始。

If a goalkeeper who has taken a goal clearance correctly intentionally touches the ball with his hand after it has left the penalty area before another player has touched it, the referees, in addition to awarding a direct free kick to the opposing team, may take disciplinary action against him in accordance with the Futsal Laws of the Game.

If the goalkeeper takes the goal clearance with his foot, the referees will issue a warning and order him to take it with his hand, but the four-second count continues from where it was stopped once the goalkeeper is ready to retake it.

If a goalkeeper, as part of a playing movement, ends up outside his goal or he or any other player end up outside the pitch, the opposing goalkeeper may take a goal clearance quickly.

If the goalkeeper takes a goal clearance and the ball crosses his goal line without first leaving the penalty area, the referees order the goal clearance to be retaken, but the four-second count continues from where it was stopped once the goalkeeper is ready to retake it.

If, when taking a goal clearance, the ball hits one of the referees inside the penalty area without first leaving the area and enters into play, the referees take no action.

如果守门员正确地将球掷出罚球区后，在其他队员触及之前故意用手触球，裁判员除判给对方球队直接任意球外，还可根据室内五人制足球竞赛规则对该队员进行纪律制裁。

如果守门员用脚踢球门球，裁判员将进行口头警告并令其用手掷球，而4秒计时在守门员准备好再次掷球门球时继续进行。

作为移动的一部分，当比赛停止时守门员处在本方球门之外或任何队员处在场地之外时，对方守门员可以快速掷出球门球。

如果守门员掷球门球，球在离开罚球区前越过本方球门线，裁判员应令球门球重掷，但4秒计时在守门员准备好再次掷球门球时继续进行。

如果在掷球门球时，球先击中位于罚球区内的裁判员后离开罚球区进入比赛，裁判员不应采取任何行动。

Procedures for infringements

Referees are reminded that opponents must remain at least 5m from the corner arc until the ball is in play. Where necessary, the referees must warn any player within this distance before the corner is taken and caution the player if he subsequently fails to retreat to the correct distance.

If a player, while correctly taking a corner, intentionally kicks the ball at an opponent in order to play the ball again but neither in a careless nor a reckless manner nor using excessive force, the referees must allow play to continue.

The ball must be placed inside the corner arc and is in play when it is kicked, therefore the ball does not need to leave the corner arc to be in play.

If a goalkeeper, as part of a playing movement, ends up outside his goal or he or any other player end up outside the pitch, the opposing team may take the corner quickly.

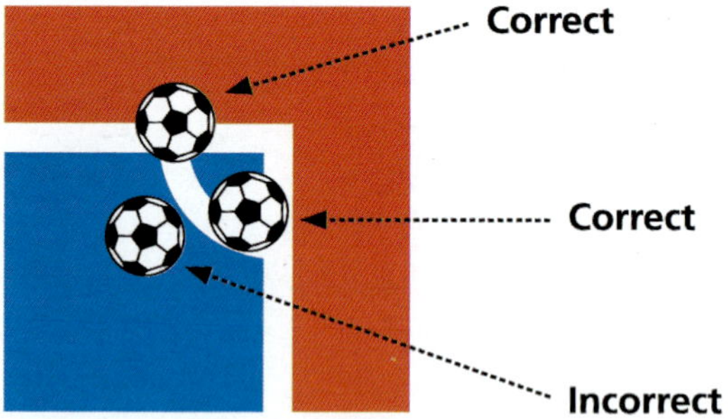

程序违规

提请裁判员注意，在角球踢出前，守方队员必须距角球弧不少于5米。当需要时，裁判员应在角球踢出前提醒任何位于规定距离内的队员，并警告随后不退出规定距离的队员。

如果队员正确地踢出角球，但却故意将球踢向对方队员以便可以第二次触球，但并不是以草率地、鲁莽地或使用过分力量的方式，则裁判员应允许比赛继续。

球必须放定在角球弧内，当球被踢时比赛即为重新开始。因此球不必离开角球弧比赛即可开始。

作为移动的一部分，当比赛停止时守门员处在本方球门之外或任何队员处在场地之外时，对方球队可快速踢出角球。

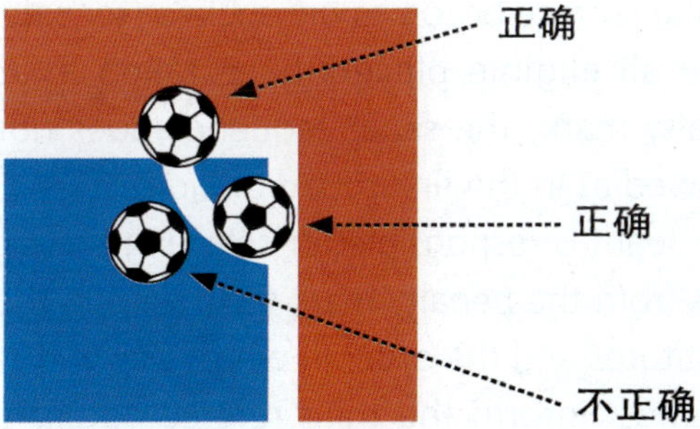

Extra time

Procedure

Procedure

- The two periods of extra time are not part of the match
- Players or substitutes may be cautioned or sent off during the two periods of extra time
- Accumulated fouls during the periods of extra time are added to those from the second half of the match
- During the periods of extra time the teams are not entitled to time-outs, even if they have not used their time-out corresponding to the second half of the match

Kicks from the penalty mark

Procedure

- The kicks from the penalty mark are not part of the match
- The penalty area where the kicks from the penalty mark are being taken may be changed only if the goal or the playing surface becomes unusable or for safety reasons
- Once all eligible players have taken a kick from the penalty mark, the same sequence does not have to be followed as in the first round of kicks
- Each team is responsible for selecting the players to take kicks from the penalty mark from among the players and substitutes and the order in which they will take the kicks and must inform the third referee before the kicks are taken

加时赛

程序

- 加时赛上、下半时不是比赛的一部分。
- 在加时赛上、下半时，队员和替补队员可被警告或罚令出场。
- 加时赛期间的累计犯规将被计入比赛下半场累计犯规中。
- 加时赛期间比赛双方没有暂停，即便该队没有使用下半场的暂停。

踢球点球决胜

程序

- 踢球点球决胜不是比赛的一部分。
- 踢球点球决胜的罚球区，只有在球门或球场表面不能正常使用或存在安全问题时可以更换。
- 当所有合法队员已经踢过球点球，接下来的顺序不必按照第一轮踢球点球的顺序进行。
- 每个队负责从队员和替补队员中挑选踢罚球点球的队员，以及他们踢球点球的顺序，并必须在踢球点球前通知第三裁判员。

- With the exception of the goalkeeper, once the kicks from the penalty mark have started, an injured player may not be replaced by an ineligible player, if there are any
- If the goalkeeper is sent off during the kicks from the penalty mark, he may be replaced by an eligible player, but not by another goalkeeper if he was excluded from taking the kicks from the penalty mark
- A player or substitute may be cautioned or sent off during the taking of kicks from the penalty mark
- The referees must not abandon the series of kicks from the penalty mark if a team is reduced to fewer than three players during the taking of kicks from the penalty mark
- If a player is injured or sent off during the taking of kicks from the penalty mark and the team has one player fewer, the referees should not reduce the number of players taking kicks for the other team
- An equal number of players from each team is required only at the start of the taking of kicks from the penalty mark
- If the ball hits one of the goalposts or the crossbar or the goalkeeper before crossing the goal line between the goalposts and the crossbar, the referees allow the goal
- If the ball bursts or becomes defective after striking one of the goalposts or the crossbar and enters the goal, the referees allow the goal
- If the ball bursts or becomes defective after hitting one of the goalposts or the crossbar and does not enter the goal, the referees do not order the penalty kick to be retaken and deem the penalty kick to have been taken

- 除守门员外，一旦开始踢球点球，任何受伤队员不能被其他无资格的队员替换。
- 在踢球点球决胜期间，如果守门员被罚令出场，他可由其他合法队员替换，但不能由被排除在踢球点球决胜名单之外的守门员替换。
- 在踢球点球决胜期间，队员和替补队员可被警告或罚令出场。
- 在踢球点球决胜期间，当一队人数减少至3人以下，裁判员不必终止踢球点球决胜。
- 在踢球点球决胜过程中，如果一名队员受伤或被罚令出场使他的队比对方少一人，裁判员不必让另一队减去一人。
- 两队人数相同的要求仅仅是在踢球点球决胜之前。
- 如果在球越过球门柱和横梁之间的球门线之前触及其中一个门柱或横梁或守门员，裁判员应判进球有效。
- 如果球在击中其中一个球门柱或横梁并进入球门后破裂或破损，裁判员应判进球有效。
- 如果球在击中其中一个球门柱或横梁但没有进入球门后破裂或破损，裁判员不应判重踢球点球，而应视该球点球已经踢过。

- If the competition rules require kicks from the penalty mark to determine the winner of a match or home-and-away and the teams refuse to do so, the referees report the incident to the relevant authorities
- If, before the penalty kicks start, one or more eligible players leave the pitch or refuse to take the penalty kicks once these have started and are not injured, the referees abandon the taking of kicks from the penalty mark and inform the relevant authorities
- During the taking of the penalty kicks, the referees do not allow cameras or other media on the pitch

- 如果竞赛规程要求通过踢球点球决定一场或主客场比赛的胜负，而相关球队拒绝执行，裁判员应向相关机构报告。
- 如果一名或多名合法队员在踢球点球决胜开始之前离开比赛场地，或在开始后拒绝踢球点球，只要他们没有受伤，裁判员可终止踢球点球决胜并通知相关机构。

- 在踢球点球决胜期间，裁判员不应允许摄影器材或其他媒体人员进入场地。

图书在版编目(CIP)数据

室内五人制足球竞赛规则. 2014 ~ 2015 / 中国足球协会审定 . -北京：人民体育出版社，2015（2019.1.重印）
ISBN 978-7-5009-4740-0

Ⅰ.①室… Ⅱ.①中… Ⅲ.①足球运动-竞赛规则-2014 ~ 2015 Ⅳ.①G843.7

中国版本图书馆 CIP 数据核字(2014)第 300687 号

*

人民体育出版社出版发行
北京中科印刷有限公司印刷
新 华 书 店 经 销

*

850×1168 32 开本 12.5 印张 230 千字
2015 年 3 月第 1 版 2019 年 1 月第 5 次印刷
印数：15,001—18,000 册

*

ISBN 978-7-5009-4740-0
定价：49.00 元

社址：北京市东城区体育馆路 8 号（天坛公园东门）
电话：67151482（发行部） 邮编：100061
传真：67151483 邮购：67118491
网址：www.sportspublish.cn
（购买本社图书，如遇有缺损页可与邮购部联系）